ENDORSEMENTS

While most focus fairly consistently on the "things" outside our lives, Antonio Baldovinos is challenging the divine encounter with Him. The spiritual kingdom within us is only as viable as one's intimacy with Jesus; Antonio makes this clear. Part of the vacuum the Lord created in the human heart is really eternal, the center being of an individual. And, the aching need for the infinite. Individuals today often find inner peace difficult, for focus is the pleasures of the world. Antonio points toward the interior pleasures that satisfy: communion with the living Savior, living in the word of God, and developing the legacy of God's will. He points the reader to the true Author of destiny. The authenticity of God's love speaks to the reader. His overwhelming presence becomes the passion as one reads and digests the important and salient points of this book. Antonio points out that it is the humble heart, the seeking heart that finds peace and significance in the internal spiritual work of God.

TOM PHILLIPS, Vice President
Billy Graham Evangelistic Association

This book is a must-read! There is no more important key to victory in the Christian life than learning to live from the inside out. This vital principle has been lost in the modern church, causing many to live without the fullness of God.

MARK ANDERSON, President
GPN/Call2All

2/0/-

The very title of this book is a prophetic word to this generation. In the midst of an hour in the church where many believers define their lives and their impact merely on what is happening on the outside, God is raising up voices like Antonio Baldovinos to call us to spend the majority of our time, strength, and energy on the building of our interior life. We are moving into days of great glory and great crisis, and the only churches and people who will be able to navigate and thrive will be the ones who have focused on the inside above the outside. My prayer is that this book will awaken a whole generation to this reality.

COREY RUSSELL, Senior Leader
International House of Prayer Kansas City

Antonio Baldovinos's *Living from the Inside Out* leads readers into better understanding and more fully experiencing just exactly what it is to commune with our heavenly Father on every level at all times. The insights, revelations, experiences, and perspectives Antonio shares invite you into a lifestyle of intimacy and encounter with Him who is *love*. Within these pages is the potential to not only deepen your relationship with the Lord, but also your relationship with the world around you as you come to better understand and more fully experience the existence of He who dwells within you, and allow Him to bring forth the fullness of what He has made available to us through the finished work of the Cross—my most favorite message in the whole Bible!

PATRICIA KING
XPmedia.com

The world always measures success by outward increase, but God always measures success by inward increase. That is why my good friend Antonio Baldovinos's new book, *Living from the Inside Out,* will stand as a pillar of truth for this generation and the generations to come. It is dripping with practical instruction and prophetic insight that will awaken a deep hunger in readers to return to their First Love. Read this book and fall in love with your Father who is in secret, and your Father who sees what is done in secret will reward you!

Rick Pino
Heart of David Worship Center

Living by faith—biblically speaking—is to "walk by faith, and not by sight." Remaining unaffected by what we see can be a challenge, especially when what we see opposes what we believe by faith. It is in these battle moments that we choose to live from the inside out, and not the other way around. Antonio writes with practical insight and spiritual depth to address the walk of faith in a 21st century context. In this book you will find helpful perspectives and revelatory keys to overcoming in faith. Antonio is an equipping teacher, and I know this book will strengthen and encourage you.

Matt Tapley, Senior Leader
Lakemount Worship Centre
Grimsby, Ontario, Canada

Antonio communicates such valuable treasures right from the heart of God—the God who created us to have communion and close relationship with Him. He's looking for friends He can confide in, those who will walk in the fear of the Lord (Psalm 25:14). I believe Antonio and his wife, Christelle, are becoming those who are known as friends of God. I have watched their lives, and they are walking what they talk. God has given them much revelation as they have researched and waited on God. I highly recommend this book.

Donna Ruth Jordan
Co-founder, YWAM Associates
International Speaker

In this anointed book, *Living from the Inside Out,* Antonio Baldovinos masterfully unveils the secret to Spirit-directed living. As he takes you on a journey through the pages of both the Old and New

Testaments, you will come to realize that it is not really a secret, but a truth that our loving Father has been revealing to humankind since the beginning of time.

REV. BILL PRANKARD, President
Bill Prankard Evangelistic Association

The moment I started to read *Living from the Inside Out,* I couldn't put it down. In every chapter I felt an invitation to go deeper with God. This book is a call to those who are not satisfied with mediocre Christianity, and who want to truly walk with God.

SAMUEL ROBINSON, Founder
Voice of Revival Ministries

As Paul commended Titus and Timothy and his fellow workers to the churches and to the people of God, I want to commend Antonio Baldovinos to you. He was born into and nurtured by a godly, missionary family. In order to sustain such a family on the front lines of missions, they had to learn the secrets of living from the inside out. Now for the past years Antonio and his family have been living out a missionary life in Youth With A Mission (YWAM), interceding, discipling, and leading many. They continue to carry on global and local ministry in the wisdom, experience, and anointing of generations. Through his writing you will receive understanding and Holy Spirit revelation for your walk. This book can change your life.

LOREN CUNNINGHAM
Founder, Youth With A Mission

Our Creator has designed us all with one fundamental and essential purpose in mind—to know Him intimately, and in so doing to enjoy Him eternally. It is only in pursuing this one thing that we can begin to reach the heights of our potential as divine image bearers and touch the depths of our capacity for the indwelling Spirit of God. In a culture saturated with "How to Do" books, I believe Antonio Baldovinos's new book, *Living from the Inside Out,* gives a much needed perspective from his own personal experience and the Word of God on "How to Be." It is a must-read for everyone who has the courage to pursue the depths of God's heart and not come up for air until...

COREY STARK, Executive Leader
International House of Prayer Kansas City

LIVING
FROM THE
INSIDE
OUT

OTHER DESTINY IMAGE BOOKS BY ANTONIO BALDOVINOS

Relentless Pursuit

LIVING
FROM THE
INSIDE
OUT

igniting a life of intimacy with God

ANTONIO BALDOVINOS

DESTINY IMAGE® PUBLISHERS, INC.

P.O. Box 310, Shippensburg, PA 17257-0310

"Promoting Inspired Lives"

This book and all other Destiny Image, Revival Press, MercyPlace, Fresh Bread, Destiny Image Fiction, and Treasure House books are available at Christian bookstores and distributors worldwide.

Cover design by: Prodigy Pixel

For more information on foreign distributors, call 717-532-3040.

Reach us on the Internet: www.destinyimage.com.

ISBN 13 TP: 978-0-7684-0463-0

ISBN 13 Ebook: 978-0-7684-0464-7

For Worldwide Distribution, Printed in the U.S.A.

1 2 3 4 5 6 7 8 / 18 17 16 15 14

DEDICATION

I dedicate this book to my children: Michael, Gabriel, Elijah, Isabella, and Justice. I had you in mind when I wrote this book. This is the best and only way to live—living from the inside out! Your mother and I love you and we are incredibly privileged to be able to be part of your lives. We love every minute!

Love,

Dad

ACKNOWLEDGMENTS

After writing a book, you realize how many people have influenced, impacted, and helped you along the way. There are too many people to name here.

I consider myself the richest man in the world. True riches and favor come only from God. He has esteemed me with His treasure, with you, Christelle. I could not garner this treasure on my own. Proverbs 18:22 (New Living Translation) says, *"The man who finds a wife finds a treasure, and he receives favor from the LORD."* At 14 years old I proposed to you as a dare. From that day on I pursued you; and at age 19 you became my wife. I am highly favored of God and rich because we get to share our lives together. I love you beyond written words. Thank you for your support in writing this book and helping me with endless hours of discussion, reading, researching, editing, and simply being by my side. You're the dream I get to live out!

On our living room wall, we have a Bible verse that says, *"Children are an inheritance from the Lord. They are a reward from Him. Like arrows in the hand of a warrior are children born in one's youth"* (Ps. 127:3-4 paraphrased). My children are a reward and an inheritance for eternity. I specifically had you, my kids, in mind when I wrote this book. May you learn and remember that living from the inside out is the best way to live—with God living on the inside affecting everything around you on the outside. May all the days of your lives be full of His wisdom, grace, and strength. My greatest prayer is that you would be extravagant lovers of Jesus and do great exploits for Him!

In one of the chapters I speak about fathers, and it made me reflect on my own father, Carlos. You have been such a great father to me and a magnificent reflection of our heavenly Father. My mother, Sandra, you highly encouraged (pushed) me into the things of God, and I am forever grateful. You taught me how to pray, read the Word, and more than anything see how much God loves me. You also inspired me to start writing as a 14-year-old. You taught me to put my heart on paper whether it was for Jesus or Christelle. I love writing. Thank you to the both of you for championing me, helping me, and loving me! I love you.

I asked a few close friends to look at the content of some of the chapters. I would like to thank Corey Stark, Eddie Boasso, Matt Tapley, Ian Byrd, Mark Anderson, and Rick Pino for looking over and speaking into part of this message. I'm very grateful for you.

This book is not possible without many people helping to make it readable. I would like to thank Kirsten Mark, Leslie Rasmussen, and Crystal Sheren for spending time editing.

Ryan Daw and John Ross, thank you for your help in designing websites and video promotions and so many other things. You bring so much to life and I appreciate your friendship!

I want to thank Mechele Wachnuk for helping take the load of so many things while I wrote this book. You are a blessing to both Christelle and I.

If I had to choose between a person who has either anointing or skill, I would choose anointing time and again. But when someone is excellent in skill and anointed in that skill, that is a huge blessing. Jeff and Mary Printz are both skilled and anointed. Thank you for your diligence and hard work in polishing up this message through your excellent editing. You have been a breath of fresh air to me!

I never dreamt that I would write books, but Destiny Image Publishing has helped make that a reality. I would like to thank the Destiny Image team for all your work in bringing forth this message.

To those who partner with Christelle and I in our ministry: I am so grateful for you. Some of you have been with us since we first started in ministry at 21 years old. Thank you for your faithfulness and partnership in sharing the Gospel!

CONTENTS

FOREWORD

You have opened the pages of a book filled with life-changing treasures. Antonio Baldovinos is one of the foremost authors, of today and from any generation. In my estimation, he is on his way to becoming a modern-day A.W. Tozer.

The world of today is filled with sound bites and microwave moments. Baldovinos points out the necessity of meditating on God's Word. The title of this book says it in a nutshell, "We are to live from the inside out." Too often our reality is set by life's circumstances and challenges. Therefore we get defeated on every turn, not by the truth of God's eternal will, but temporal things and the painful fiery darts of the enemies' attacks.

However, over and over in this exciting book full of truth, we are reminded of God's original design for us as His children. God longs to walk and talk with us in an intimate setting; this was always His desire for us. Posing the question, "Can this first relationship be restored?" *Living from the Inside Out* cries out with a resounding YES!

As I read its pages I thought back to moments with my own two children and five, almost six grandchildren. Those memories brought a resonance of warm emotions. The joy that shoots through me as the little grandchildren shout, "Nonnie!" when they first see me, I feel so celebrated and loved! God receives that kind of divine pleasure from us,

His children, when we enter His presence with the same lifting up of our hands in joy!

He is our Abba Father! The truth of this is found in these pages in an amplified version.

Just as it takes time in a natural relationship to maintain intimate freshness, so does our relationship with the Word of God. I found myself falling more deeply in love with my Father through the pages of this book. In fact, you will do the same yourself.

It seems that the Holy Spirit is saying to many today, *"Come away, My beloved."*

He is wooing us with His own love songs, giving intimate seasons of drinking deeply of His presence through worship and the Word. What a mixture! Reading the Word and meditating upon it gives food to our hungry hearts and water to our thirsty souls in the midst of the crisis and shaking that surrounds us.

My heart found a new song as I read the pages of *Living from the Inside Out*—and so will yours. Be refreshed by the revelation you will find chapter by chapter; the Lover of your soul awaits. Prepare to be awed by God!

CINDY JACOBS
Generals International
Dallas, Texas

THE CASTLE WITHIN

I abruptly awoke from a dream the weekend of our annual Pursuit Conference in 2011. This book, *Living from the Inside Out,* is the reality of that divine encounter, and as you read this account I hope it will inspire you to take a journey in exploring your heart and identity—plunging you into God's original purpose for your life to commune with Him deeply and intimately.

As the dream began, I saw myself in a beautiful, majestic castle at the foot of a mountain surrounded by luscious gardens and tall trees. The outside walls, with towers at each corner, were thick and seemed to reach the sky. A sparkling blue river flowed in through the front gate.

As I neared the entrance, my heart began to pound and I felt compelled to walk faster and explore past the tall wooden gates. The intensity increased as I sensed I might discover what I was tirelessly searching for my whole life.

Because the gate was wide open and I entered the seemingly impenetrable fortress with such ease, I wondered why I had been living outside the gates most of my life, venturing past them into the outer court only a few times before. I lived a busy and distracted existence and spent most of my time outside the walls. I rarely, if ever, noticed the castle or even considered I could enter and explore freely.

Now all I could see was this immense fortress, and I was drawn to move closer and satisfy my curiosity. I encountered the large castle doors, and my eyes were opened to see the magnificence and intricacies of the structure. The hand-carved wooden doors were elaborately crafted with great detail. Above the archway was a large iron plaque with the inscription *Antonio Baldovinos.* I was stunned and thought, *What is my name doing there?* My heart beat faster and I drew a deep breath as I slowly pushed open the heavy door and peered inside. The enormous height of the inner walls was truly breathtaking and the sparkling beauty of the inner court incredible. The floor was made of smooth rare stones carefully placed to complement and accentuate each other. I could scarcely comprehend the splendor and began to realize this castle was uniquely made for me.

I quickly explored each room. Everything was ornate and fashioned with great care—high windows with bright light streaming in; large stone fireplaces; libraries with floor-to-ceiling shelves lined with books; a polished, gleaming dining hall; massive bedchambers; elegant ballrooms; and courtyards with flourishing gardens, fruitful vineyards, and running streams. Each room was more beautiful than the last. The deeper I ventured, the more peaceful and intimate the surroundings became. Despite the great beauty of the inner courts and rooms, I knew I had not yet found what I was looking for. I felt drawn to the inner chamber where I instinctively knew the King resided.

Awaking from this vivid dream I knew God was calling me closer to Him. He wanted me to live differently and explore areas I had previously ignored. I had lived much of my life from the outside in, letting physical realities lead me. God wanted me to reside with Him in the inner chamber—the Holy of Holies. That castle represented my life, and He was waiting for me to accept the invitation to fully encounter the God who resides in me.

～⌣～

You are also a castle and originally designed with a glorious and splendid outer gate, inner court, and Holy of Holies—not to mention many beautiful rooms and gardens. What a breathtaking reality! We are the habitation of the King! He wants to be so near us and make His home within us so we can live from that place of strength.

Most believers remain in the outer courts of the Christian life, rarely venturing past the gates let alone exploring the inner courts and reaching the place of true intimacy with God. They don't know what the castle looks like on the inside—its many rooms made with great care and exquisite beauty and detail. They settle for a place outside the wall, unaware of the invitation to enter.

It's time to stop living from the outside, focusing solely on our physical bodies. It's time to start exploring the reason we were created: to commune with God at the deepest levels and live from the inner chamber; to enter the Holy of Holies and dine with the King who lives within us, sharing the most secret and sacred parts of our lives.

A.W. Tozer, one of my favorite authors, writes, "A spiritual kingdom lies all about us, enclosing us, embracing us, altogether within reach of our inner selves, waiting for us to recognize it. God Himself is here waiting our response to His presence. This eternal world will come alive to us the moment we begin to reckon upon its reality."[1]

I have lived so much of my life unaware this castle existed for me to explore. To open the door, walk through the glorious gates and gardens, and go to the inner place, it was essential I posture my heart to truly commune with God—committing to seek knowledge of the One who fashioned and created me.

I invite you to explore with me, discover this interior life, and begin to live from the inside out.

Chapter 1

VISION TO LIVE FROM THE INSIDE OUT

The interior journey of the soul from the wilds of
sin into the enjoyed presence of God is beautiful…
Ransomed men need no longer pause in fear before
the Holy of Holies. God wills that we should push
on into His presence and live our whole life there.
—A.W. TOZER, *The Pursuit of God*

Is this seriously all there is to life? This can't be the life that Christ died for. I know there is more, but I do not know how to get it. I know I am missing something, but I do not know what it is. Do these thoughts sound familiar to you? What if I were to tell you that most people are living their lives upside down and outside in? Would you know what I'm talking about?

Do you remember when your dad or mom told you that your shirt was inside out and you didn't realize it until you looked? You had a choice at that moment to see that the stitches and the seams were inside out and flip the shirt around. Or you could continue to walk around with the shirt inside out. The decision was completely up to you. It is time to not just look at the way we live, but it is time to change it!

These questions and others like them ring true to your heart because you inherently know what I am talking about. You know by nature that this life and its cares and pleasures pass away. You know this not because someone told you, but because you are on the same search that I am, along with the rest of humanity. This is the search that God placed inside of us. God put eternity on humankind's mind and filled the human heart with longing. Truthfully, we do not know all that we long for, until we see the magnificent God.

> *He has also set eternity in the human heart; yet no one can fathom what God has done from beginning to end* (Ecclesiastes 3:11 NIV).

> *...he marked out their appointed times in history and the boundaries of their lands. God did this so that they would seek him and perhaps reach out for him and find him, though he is not far from any one of us* (Acts 17:26-27 NIV).

We were made in such a way so that we would find God. He wanted us so much that He put the desires within us that He knew only He could fulfill. He placed a God-aimed search engine in our heart so we would search and search until through the seeking we find the very answer to the cry of our soul—*Him!* No matter how noble or selfish a pursuit may be, nothing casts a shadow on the unsurpassable greatness of knowing the very God who created us. The awe, splendor, intimacy, love, terror, joy, and peace that we want are all found in Him.

We may hear this and know it intellectually, yet we continue on the race of life rarely allowing, if ever, ourselves to be consumed with the fire and passion of God we were made to encounter. We think too lowly of God; we do not know who He really is. He is the living flame of love and all-consuming fire. He longs to consume us and be our heart's desire. He wants to satisfy us beyond our wildest dreams.

In this book I hope to point you toward the God who fills these longings and in His very person is, *"your exceedingly great reward"* (Gen. 15:1). Imagine that! He is so incredible that nothing can trump the reward of Himself. History is laced with men and women who abandoned it all because they found their exceedingly great reward in Him.

More Christians today are interested in the world around them than in the eternal God within them. God eternal is living inside them and has infinite, glorious riches available for them. However, we are so distracted with lesser things that most will never even take the time to look and see that we have been living our lives from the outside in, instead of from the inside out.

True living is living from the inside out. If we can take hold of this truth, that every desire and every longing can be satisfied, we would stop at nothing to have it! We would then say like Paul, *"I have suffered the loss of all things, and count them as rubbish, that I may gain Christ"* (Phil. 3:8).

PURPOSE IN VISION

Where there is no prophetic vision the people cast off restraint... (Proverbs 29:18 ESV).

When our hearts exist in a void of illumined sight and vision, we quickly cast off restraint and stray into hopelessness, despair, and disappointment. Seeing clearly with perspective will steady our gaze, strengthen us to persevere, and hem us into a life of wisdom, free from vain and worthless pursuits. Allowing us freedom to enjoy true life from the inside out.

Throughout this book my intent is to introduce you to the subject of communion with God. Let me define what I mean to "commune" with God. Commune means: *eating of God, dining with Him, to communicate intimately.* We are invited to eat and drink of Him, to drink the water in which we will never thirst again. To commune is to partake of Him at the deepest level. To know Him to the extent He can be known, to be constantly searching, seeking, and finding. To be eating, drinking to satisfaction, yet hungering for more. Jesus said to the woman at the well, *"…whoever drinks of the water that I shall give him will never thirst. But the water that I shall give him will become in him a fountain of water springing up into everlasting life"* (John 4:14).

I hope to inspire you to pursue and establish a vision for this that will serve as a plumb line for your life. The greatest desire in my life is to know God for myself and go into the depths of God to the fullest extent of His grace. I wasn't made for anything else other than communion with the uncreated God. You were fashioned with an infinite purpose and desire for an infinite God, and you don't have to wait until heaven to experience and take hold of it. You can grasp it now!

OUR CONDITION

Thomas Dubay confirms this inner longing and desire stating the fact that:

> You and I, each one of us without exception, can be defined as an aching need for the infinite. Some people realize this and some do not. But even the latter illustrates this inner ache when, not having God deeply, they incessantly spill themselves out into excitements and experiences, licit or illicit. They are trying to fill their inner emptiness, but they never succeed, which is why the search is incessant. Though worldly pleasure seeking never fulfills and satisfies in a continuing way, it may tend momentarily to distract and to dull the profound pain of the inner void. If these people allow themselves a moment of reflective silence (which they seldom do), they notice a still, small voice whispering, "Is this all there is?" They begin to

sense a thirst to love with abandon, without limit, without end, without lingering aftertastes of bitterness.[1]

All of humanity has the same inner ache for the infinite; whether Christian or not, we can be defined as having this vast, gaping need in all of us. There is a fundamental hunger for communion with the infinite God that absolutely nothing else can fulfill. Unfortunately, people may not realize that nothing can satisfy their hunger until they have tasted and have experienced and know the love of Father God, the satisfaction and fulfillment of their inner longing. For many of you and millions of others have proved this to be true. *What else is there?* What else is left, when you know that in every place you have searched you inevitably keep coming up short? It is time to stop looking in all the wrong places.

In this day and age we diagnose our need for fascination and consider our options. We look to entertainment, fame, power, work, money, or relationships. We may even turn to religion. Even religion only deals with the external conditions instead of the heart. I see a vast explosion of herculean social service projects. Even while the great feelings of helping lingers, it leaves an inward frustration and possibly feelings of bitterness. We try everything, but our efforts all fall short of the true life we were meant to live.

> *So I tell you this, and insist on it in the Lord, that you must no longer live as the Gentiles do, in the futility of their thinking. They are darkened in their understanding and separated from the life of God because of the ignorance that is in them due to the hardening of their hearts. Having lost all sensitivity, they have given themselves over to sensuality so as to indulge in every kind of impurity, and they are full of greed* [with a continual lust for more] (Ephesians 4:17-19 NIV).

"More, more, more" has become the motto of a restless and discontent generation. The endless options offered in our nation have risen into an industry committed to feeding the lusts of men. Everything must be faster, bigger, and brighter—a new restaurant with bigger portions and better atmospheres, a new blend of coffee with better flavor, a television with a clearer picture, a cell phone with added features, a newer and a faster car. On and on it goes, and yet no one stops to consider the insanity inherent in the endless pursuit of more.[2]

The opening scenes in the Bible display the Lord was walking in the midst of the garden, calling out to Adam, "Where are you?" Adam had a face-to-face relationship with God. We were fashioned for this very reason—to be in fellowship with Him, to have an unhindered relationship with God like Adam had in the garden.

Adam chose for all humankind the way of selfishness and pride. He was fooled, but he still chose, therefore separating us from the life of God.

Just like Adam, we have a choice as to whether we will honor the One who created us and why we were created. We have to choose whether we will love God with everything in us, or not love Him at all. We must understand that there is nothing we can do to change the way we were fashioned. To those who love God, this is glorious; yet to those who hate Him, this truth is profoundly offensive. This truth makes war or peace in the heart. No matter how violently people may try to assert their independence and autonomy, they can never purge from their souls the yearning need for God in order to be complete.

SEARCHING BUT NEVER FINDING

People keep looking in places that will never satisfy. It goes on and on and on, a continual living from the outside in, chasing every type of physical and emotional pleasure that never satisfies.

On and on humanity goes in its feeding frenzy, devouring anything within its reach that promises some measure of gratification. Yet in the folly of a hamster on its wheel, regardless of variety or volume of consumption, the torrent of want cannot be quelled and the gnawing ache persists. The unprecedented abundance of resource together with the rise of the techno-logical age has created an environment that has awakened the incessant want of the human soul in heightened measure.[3]

HOUR OF DECISION

I believe we are in a critical hour of decision. We are standing on the precipice of the ages. We must grapple with the reality of the time we are living in. There is a line drawn in the sand. We are nearing the end of the age, and we have to look to see if we are prepared and if we have oil in our lamps. This *oil* that I'm talking about represents the presence of God within us. Let me show you this in Scripture.

> *Then the kingdom of heaven shall be likened to ten virgins who took their lamps and went out to meet the bridegroom. Now five of them were wise, and five were foolish. Those who were foolish took their lamps and took no oil with them, but the wise took oil in their vessels with their lamps. But while the bridegroom was delayed, they all slumbered and slept. And at midnight a cry was heard: "Behold, the bride-groom is coming; go out to meet him!"* (Matthew 25:1-6)

I agree with Stephen Venable when he asks,

Do we have enough reality in our soul to withstand the onslaught of distraction and seduction by the spirit of the age now when all of the options are before us?

Do we have enough interior pleasure to withstand the temp-tation and testing of the end of the age when there is nothing available in the natural arena to partake of? These are the ques-tions of Matthew 25. Will we have oil in our lamps in the midnight hour of history as the Bridegroom draws near? Will we have the reality of love burning on the inside or will we find only bareness within us?[4]

Vision for Communion

Communion is the place of encounter. "Communion is the place in which these two movements, His desire to satisfy us and our desire for Him, converge in the realm of our experience."[5] You see, heaven invades earth upon the surrender of our lives to Jesus. This surrender invites the God of heaven to reside in our inner self. This is when life really begins. Sadly, so many people have not tried communion; or a better way to say it, they have not experienced heaven. And let me tell you, heaven is a real place.

> *To them God willed to make known what are the riches of the glory of this mystery…which is Christ in you, the hope of glory* (Colossians 1:27).

Friend, this is what our flesh is demanding. Clearly, this is what we have been looking for all along. Even if you have encountered God at some point but have become distracted by sin, complacency, compromise, or simply the busyness of life, this is exactly what the need and craving of our hearts is and what we need to re-sign up to pursue. It's not good enough to just have ideas about God stirred up, we have to come in contact with the living God and have experiential knowledge of Him from the inside. It's not good enough to only attend a sweet worship event or a speaker-packed conference or even read a good book about God. We desperately need a personal encounter that erupts from personal devotion and worship.

I'm not talking about a bunch of hype that is frantic in some sort of worship service that is only outward in appearance. The one-time "hit" is only surface. I'm talking about the ecstasy that fills your very soul with the beauty and glory of God that lives in you. I am talking about your eyes being enlightened and you able to see Him and commune with Him for yourself. I am talking about being fascinated with God either for the first time or once again. This is the best life!

J.I. Packer, in his book *Knowing God,* says, "Once you become aware that the main business that you are here for is to know God, most of life's problems fall into place of their own accord."[6] Once we come to searching the depths of God, all the big issues in our life fall to the wayside. They seem so insignificant to knowing and searching out God. A.W. Tozer says, "The man who comes to a right belief about God is relieved of ten thousand temporal problems."[7]

YOU ARE HIS ENDLESS DESIRE

But now in Jesus Christ you who once were far off have been brought near... (Ephesians 2:13).

The best part about knowing that we desire God is that we are uniquely made in His image to bear His likeness and character. God, the Creator of desire and the Creator of humankind, desires us too. It would be safe to say that we don't have the slightest clue how much He desires us. We must see that deep communion with Him was and is initiated by Him. This is not something we are trying to convince Him to allow. "For the first time in our lives we truly touch the bliss of entering into the purpose for which we were created. Most people spend their entire lives in futility, desperately spilling themselves out upon all the world has to offer in an attempt to answer the ache within them."[8]

At that day you will know that I am in My Father, and you in Me, and I in you (John 14:20).

The Father was willing to send His beloved Son who in turn was willing to give us His life unto death. This shows the intense passion and explicit desire that He had for us in times past and the desire He still has today.

> In Him there is no absence but only presence, no vacancy but only fullness. Thus, we know that He did not create humanity out of His need but out of His desire.

> Somewhere in the depths of God's being, He has reserved room for this ordained desire—the desire that He would dwell with man. The Creator desires to bring the created into the communion shared between Father, Son, and Holy Spirit. His determined desire is to bring us into the fullness of His embrace, the plentitude of love within the Godhead.[9]

One of my favorite descriptive titles of God is the *"Desire of All Nations,"* which is found in Haggai 2:7. He is the anticipation of all creation waiting to be inhabited by their Creator. We are His desire and He is our desire! God is the desire of all people groups and all people groups will eventually desire Him. Most people don't realize God's desire for us. I would also say that our desire for Him is very dim in comparison. "As created beings we cannot have a desire or longing that is beyond His reach. We can try to fulfill it in a wrong way, but by nature we cannot desire something He did not intend to be filled. Indeed, we often want far too little."[10]

Even when thinking about the word "desire," let's not get confused with a mild definition, such as desiring a cup of water to quench your thirst. "The word 'desire' covers a wide range of human wants, emotions, and cravings."[11] It is the strong feeling of wishing and wanting something. Our soul's desires will only be satisfied by Him.

> Our desire for God is but an echo and participation in His own desire. Every longing for God we ever experience is held within the Great Desire of the God Man Jesus. We desire

God because He first desired us. We long because He longs. Every desire we have for Him is not from our own heart but from His. Longing is the agreement of our beings with the heart of God. When we enter into our inheritance of this desiring God, we are participating in what has always been in His heart.[12]

The great paradox is that He establishes in us the desire that He intends to satisfy. He gives the desire for Him, draws us to Him, and is the only One who can fill that longing for Him.

Made for Communion

In whom you also are being built together for a dwelling place [habitation] of God in the Spirit (Ephesians 2:22).

I will set My tabernacle among you, and My soul shall not abhor you. I will walk among you and be your God, and you shall be My people (Leviticus 26:11-12).

For the LORD your God walks in the midst of your camp, to deliver you and give your enemies over to you; therefore your camp shall be holy, that He may see no unclean thing among you, and turn away from you (Deuteronomy 23:14).

I hope that we can see as we look at these Scriptures, it is "consistent that God is unrelenting in His desire for relational nearness with His people. As members of the body of Christ, each one of us without exception possesses an indescribable treasure on the inside of us that we must understand and learn to recognize. For indeed, this treasure is a personal presence, and our invitation is to commune with Him deeply."[13]

God didn't just want to walk near us, as in the days of Moses with cloud by day and a fire by night. He made a sacred space for us to commune with Him on the inside. It was His unimaginable desire to be as close to us as possible, whether we realize it or not. Most will not reach out for Him, in response to Him, but that does not change the fact that we have been made for this type of communion.

God never wanted to just be *near* humankind. He didn't just want to rest upon us either. He wanted to dwell *within* us through the indwelling Holy Spirit. He went from walking in communion with Adam and Eve in the cool of the day, the original perfect state He created, to a less than perfect state when even the Word of the Lord was rarely heard in the land, as in the days of Samuel (see 1 Sam. 3:1). He set forth prophets and kings to speak and lead His people, a position He always wanted for Himself. He desired to speak to His people, not have someone speak on His behalf. And He didn't want someone else to lead His people; He wanted to be that Person.

To emphasize that point, Richard J. Foster, in his book *Celebration of Discipline,* says,

> Human beings seem to have a perpetual tendency to have somebody else talk to God for them. We are content to have the message secondhand. One of Israel's fatal mistakes was their insistence upon having a human king rather than resting in the theocratic rule of God over them. We can detect a note of sadness in the Word of the Lord, "They have rejected me from being king over them" (1 Sam. 8:7). The history of religion is the story of an almost desperate scramble to have a king, a mediator, a priest, a pastor, a go-between."[14]

God started in the garden desiring intimacy; He desired it in Samuel's day and He desires this still. He wants communion with you. When I speak about communion, I am speaking of nearness. His heart is tender toward His people, always holy and majestic. For those walking in sin, there should be fear, but for those with a broken and contrite heart, He cannot refuse them (see Ps. 51:10-11).

INDWELLING SPIRIT

The first step we must take to understanding the indwelling Spirit of God is to know that Jesus died for this very thing. His endless desire to have closeness and nearness was first in His mind. We also must realize that if we have given our lives to Jesus Christ, it is not a force or an influence that has inhabited us. It is the third Person of the Trinity who has come and taken residence within us. Holy Spirit, we welcome you.

> *I denied myself nothing my eyes desired; I refused my heart no pleasure. My heart took delight in all my labor and this was the reward for all my toil. Yet when I surveyed all that my hands had done and what I had toiled to achieve, everything was meaningless, a chasing after the wind; nothing was gained under the sun* (Ecclesiastes 2:10-11 NIV).

This entire book is laced with the thread of one purpose and consistently presents one theme—to attract us to commune with God. To that, I add to this statement, two questions: What else is there to life? After searching high and low, feeding all of the physical pleasures that a soul can desire, are we ever satisfied? Solomon, who wrote Ecclesiastes, said that he *denied himself nothing that his eyes desired; he refused his heart no pleasure* (see Eccl. 2:10). But in the end Solomon called his earthly pursuits meaningless and vanity. So what's the point of life outside of communion with our Creator? Out of His good pleasure He created us to commune and dwell with Him forever (see Rev. 4:11). So if we don't respond accordingly, what are we chasing and where will it lead us?

OUR HEARTS BURNING

When he [Jesus] was at the table with them, he took bread, gave thanks, broke it and began to give it to them. Then their

*eyes were opened and they recognized him, and he disap-
peared from their sight. They asked each other, "Were not our
hearts burning within us while he talked with us on the road
and opened the Scriptures to us?"* (Luke 24:30-32 NIV)

Here we can see that the Living Word came in contact with two
men. Jesus didn't just want proximity but communion and dialogue.
Jesus revealed Himself and set these men's hearts on fire. Jesus is the
Living Word, the very representation of God's heart. The Word became
flesh, meaning that the interior of God, the secret of God's innermost
being took on human form. The Word is what sets the heart on fire.
Jesus talks to us, just like He talked to these men. God longs to talk to
us. He wants to speak the Living Word to set our hearts on fire. The
Living Word wants to open our hearts through the written Word by the
Holy Spirit.

He wants to come in contact with your heart and reveal Himself
and set your heart on fire. There is a place in your heart that when the
wood of your heart and the flame of God's presence ignite, your heart
will burn—and there will be no way you will ever be satisfied with
anything else. When you taste Him, He will be your one all-consuming desire.

HOLY INVITATION

*I have come that they may have life, and that they may have
it more abundantly* (John 10:10).

When the Word became flesh and dwelt among us, the purpose in
His heart was to secure our redemption on the cross; ultimately, His
perfect plan for us was to know Him and have nothing in the way
of experiencing the abundant life found only in Him. While this does
refer to eternal life, we often think of this gift of eternal life in terms
of length of time or duration. What about the quality of abundant life

now? I'm not talking about the possession of things, but the greatest reward of Him satisfying our longing to be with Him, and He with us. This is what I consider the greatest quality of abundant life. Jesus died that we may experience the fullness of life beyond our wildest dreams and imaginations—both now and into eternity.

I believe that throughout this book, you will hear God inviting you to encounter Him from the inside, to see Him in a new light, and to live a life with burning desire for Him and His purposes. The combination of this is communion from the inside. It is living a life where your internal reality is full of life and vibrancy and changes how you live. You will develop a hunger, thirst, and zeal for more. Nothing else will satisfy or give you the joy, love, fulfillment, and pleasure that this alone can bring. I pray that God would awaken love within and reveal Himself to you like you have never seen or known Him before. True life is living from the inside out, not from the outside in.

To conclude this chapter, I want to end by sharing the words of an amazing song called "Garden" written by Misty Edwards:

> *There's a place within,*
> *where no man can go,*
> *in the secret reservoir of the soul.*
> *In Your jealousy, You've created me*
> *as a garden enclosed*
> *for You alone.*
> *Here it's You and me alone, God.*
> *You've hedged me in*
> *with skin*
> *all around me.*
> *I'm a garden closed,*
> *a locked garden.*
> *Life takes place*
> *Behind the face,*

where it's You and me alone.
I don't want to waste my life,
living on the outside.
I'm going to live from the inside out.
So come into Your garden.[15]

Chapter 2

OUR ORIGINAL DESIGN

There is no greater discovery than seeing
God as the author of your destiny.
—Ravi Zacharias, *Walking from East to West*

For almost a decade I traveled worldwide directing evangelistic campaigns and seeing thousands of people respond to the Gospel. This has been one of the greatest privileges I have ever been part of, to see people surrender their lives and give them in exchange for the life of Jesus Christ. Those under the age of 18 years made over 80 percent of the decisions for Christ during those years. The young people I came in contact with were looking for real answers to questions from their hearts. So many people have real questions and are desperately looking for real answers. This generation is filled with "seekers." They are looking for a deeper meaning and purpose for their life.

Throughout history, people have been searching for answers to three fundamental questions. Regardless of nationality, ethnicity, or class in society, the questions are the same. We all want answers to these same three basic questions since we entered this world. Simply stated, these most common questions echoing in the minds of humankind include:

- Who am I?

- Why am I here?

- Why is there so much injustice, pain, and poverty in the world?

Throughout this chapter I hope to scratch the surface in answering these questions. My purpose is not to go into some theological discussion hoping to answer life's biggest questions, but rather to go deep in God and explore the inner chamber of humanity, which will lead to encountering the God of our being. I realize, however, I have to speak to these core questions of life in order to experience the intimate knowledge of God. I would agree with A.W. Tozer who asked another important question that brings the point home: "If a person is living just because it is the best alternative to dying, what good is it?"[1]

I am not a theologian. I am a simple man who wants to experience the fullness of God on this side of heaven with the full extent of His grace. I also know that living life from the outside focuses on my physical body and senses—and it is not all that it's cracked up to be! When I found the biggest, most exciting pleasure-seeking thrill, I am still looking for something greater and riskier to capture my attention. It is never enough! Alternately, in experiencing true life, from the inside out, and encountering the Creator of my being, I am sated, but at the same time I want more of Him.

Let me explain. When I encounter God, I am not left feeling unfulfilled, but quite the opposite. I feel like this is exactly what I was made for. Encountering God is the answer to the cry of my being. Knowing God for myself doesn't even compare to other things in life that present me with such high expectation only to find I am bored all the way through the experience.

FIGURING IT OUT

Discovering the answers to these three questions is crucial for us to go deeper in our purpose in life: *encountering God.* These three basic questions: *who am I, why am I here, and why is there so much injustice, pain and poverty in the world,* can become so complicated when asked of those who do not know God. When scholars and so-called "experts" try to answer these questions, they always come up with an incomplete conclusion because they start without God at the center. When you do not begin with the Author of all things, the Creator, it is impossible to answer even the fundamentals of life's questions, because all answers are found in God and God alone.

I agree with Misty Edwards who suggests, "If the meaning of life is found absent of God and in the goodness of humanity alone, then we are all to be pitied, because it cannot be attained or sustained."[2] She also states:

> In order to find meaning in life, we have to find purpose in death, and in order to face eternity, we must come to the conclusion about God. You will never find sufficient meaning in a vapor called life if it is not anchored in something transcendent, with eternal continuity. In other words, to find the meaning of life we must deal with God. The purpose of life, in the most universal sense, must be accessible to all, and it must have continuity into eternity. This means we have to deal with the Creator and His original intention in order to find the "why" behind the "what" of life. He is the only one who can make sense of this world we are in. He has the answers to why He created us in the first place.[3]

So let's get down to it. Those who know me best know I am a "bottom line" kind of man. I love the bottom line of things. I enjoy figuring out the process once I know the end result or destination. In

Christianity the bottom line is that when we give our lives to the lordship of Jesus, we get the kingdom of God and all its glorious mysteries on the front end, giving us the invitation and opportunity and the thrill of discovering Him and His ways for all of eternity.

The bottom line is: *you were designed and created by God, for God, and to partner with God.* He didn't need your efforts; He just wanted you to work alongside Him, simply to be with Him. God created all things for His enjoyment. There was no other purpose for creation than to fulfill God's enjoyment, for His good pleasure. God doesn't need your work, inasmuch as we don't need an ant to make an anthill, only to be blown away by the next gust of wind. Every person needs to know who he or she is and what purpose they were created for, *to fully comprehend all that God has for them. We all need a starting point in order to know where we are going.*

> Our definitions of the meaning of life must be rooted in our conclusions about eternity, or they are less than accurate and leave us empty. To find the purpose of life, we must find the purpose beyond the grace and come to the real conclusion not only about humans but also about God. We have to get caught up in His story in order to see ours.[4]

> *You are worthy, O Lord, to receive glory and honor and power; for You created all things, and by Your will [pleasure] they exist and were created* (Revelation 4:11).

God brought to life and fashioned everything! God is the Composer of the universe. When God made the birds of the air, He placed in them a little harp in their throats, covered them with feathers and said, "Now sing!" They erupted with beautiful sounds and have been singing ever since.

God created the trees to bear fruit, blessed them and made them for us to eat. God made the beasts of the field to feed and clothe humankind.

He created by His will and for His good pleasure; and when He made everything, He sat back, admired it, and said it was "good."

Now when God created man, it was the greatest day in heaven. All the angels sang with exceeding and abundant joy to celebrate the creation of humankind. They had a party over us. In Job 38:7 it even says the angels shouted for joy! A.W. Tozer puts it this way, "Man is the darling of the universe, the centerpiece of God's affection."[5] To say we are incredibly special is a gross understatement. We are the objects of God's affections; and in fact, very, very special and extraordinary. There is no other creature like us.

> *When I consider Your heavens, the work of Your fingers, the moon and the stars, which You have ordained, what is man that You are mindful of him, and the son of man that You visit him? For You have made him a little lower than the angels, and You have crowned him with glory and honor. You have made him to have dominion over the works of Your hands; You have put all things under his feet, all sheep and oxen—even the beasts of the field, the birds of the air, and the fish of the sea that pass through the paths of the seas* (Psalm 8:3-8).

In the vastness of the universe, man is very small indeed. But seen as a spiritual creature in the bosom of God, he is greater than all the winds that blow and all the mountains that rise and all the seas that flow and all the rivers that run down to the sea. He is greater, because God made him in His own image.[6]

MY FAVORITE PART

So God created man in His own image; in the image of God He created him; male and female He created them (Genesis 1:27).

Meditate on one of my favorite thoughts: *you and I look like our Father.* We were made in His likeness, in His image. The reason we feel and have emotions is because our Father does too. The reason why we have a mind full of nonstop thoughts and images is because our Creator God does too. The reason why we have longings for relationship is because our heavenly Father does too. Our Father has a family, with sons and daughters, a bride and a bridegroom, and He yearns to have His family near Him, where He is.

> God made man to be like Him so that man could give more pleasure to God than all other creatures. Only in man, as created by God, can God admire Himself. Man is the mirror image in which God looks to see Himself. Man is the reflection of the glory of God, which was the purpose and intention of God originally. Man's supreme function through all eternity is to reflect God's highest glory, and that God might look into the mirror called man and see His own glory shining there. Through man, God could reflect His glory to all creation.[7]

A Father Looks Intensely

I have seen six of my children born. Every one of the births was glorious for many reasons, but one very obvious reason is because we have something inherent in us—we want to see what our children look like. As a father, I looked intently as soon as each one of my babies was born. The first thing I would do is look at the gender; even if I knew it before, I wanted to see for myself. Then I wanted to look at every detail of their features. Immediately I looked over their wrinkly little face and body to see which attributes they received from me and what they had from Christelle. I won't lie, even though my wife is extremely beautiful, there is something deep down in me that hoped for them to have some of my features.

As the children grew, I loved hearing their first giggles, seeing their first steps, and feeling their little arms hug my neck. I loved hearing their voices and watching them mature and discover life. One of the favorite topics of discussion for Christelle and I is sharing our observations of each of our children's varying personalities. It is a fascinating thing to see what part of their personality may be like Christelle's or mine. The subject of our children never gets old to us, no matter how many kids we have been privileged to have, we have found each one to be so profoundly different, and the discovery of each one wonderful.

God is the perfect Father; and the reason we enjoy the discovery of our children is because He enjoys us this way, only much, much more. He made you and me to mirror Him; we all have varying traits and characteristics of Him. We are made to be just like our Father. We are the image of Him and He loves and delights in it. He loves looking at our personalities, our features, our unique qualities, our likes and dislikes; He loves our outbursts of joy and watching what thrills us.

The reason no human is the same as another is because we all carry aspects of God, and He is infinite. We are image bearers gloriously reflecting our Father's glory throughout our life; and the reason we are so wonderful is because we are just like Him. He is a proud Father watching His kids carry His very own attributes.

You weren't created merely to work, get an education, and aimlessly go through life looking for pleasure and happiness. You were created to be enjoyed by God; and as He touches you with who He is, you in turn are to enjoy Him.

ULTIMATE PURPOSE

The ultimate purpose for me being created was to commune with God. We will look later in the chapter about the pleasure of communing with God. You may ask, what is communion? Some may think it's the grape juice and bread pieces that you partake of at church. Communion is so much more than that. Communion is the experience of "sharing or exchanging of intimate thoughts and feelings." To commune with God is the ultimate goal of creation and is the food and water that satisfies the hunger and thirst of our soul. We were made to be fascinated and enraptured by our God. We were made for pleasure and communion.

We now have concluded that God made us, for Himself and in His image, for His pleasure. Let's look at how this got started in the first place.

Let's Start at the Beginning

In Genesis 2:8, God planted a garden in Eden and He placed man in it, but He gave man some instructions.

> *Then the Lord God took the man and put him in the garden of Eden to tend and keep it. And the Lord God commanded the man, saying, "Of every tree of the garden you may freely eat; but of the tree of the knowledge of good and evil you shall not eat, for in the day that you eat of it you shall surely die* (Genesis 2:15-17).

As the account continues we see that God made Eve out of Adam's rib in Genesis 2:21 and in verse 25 it says, *"they were both naked, the man and his wife, and were not ashamed."* We see that Adam and Eve had purity and a level of intimacy with each other that didn't affect their physical appearance at all. This is an important key to highlight, which I will explain further later on.

As they were in the garden, they were tempted to sin directly against what God had commanded them not to do. *"Of every tree of the garden you may freely eat; but of the tree of the knowledge of good and evil you shall not eat, for in the day that you eat of it you shall surely die"* (Gen. 2:16-17).

As we know, Adam and Eve did eat of that tree, but did not immediately die. Or did they? We know that they didn't die physically right away because they lived hundreds of years more. Did God lie when He said they would surely die when He commanded them not to eat of that tree? Was the serpent correct in doubting God and His claim that if they ate of that tree (of knowledge of good and evil) that they would die?

First, let's look at one of the most fascinating realities that Adam and Eve walked in. In Genesis 3:8 it says that Adam and Eve *"heard the sound of the Lord God walking in the garden in the cool of the day, and Adam and his wife hid themselves from the presence of the Lord God among the trees of the garden."*

Adam and Eve had an intimate, real, connected relationship with God. It was as real as you with your closest friend. I must also note that it seems they had regular set times when they met because God said, *"Where are you?"* to Adam and Eve. And Adam and Eve knew God was going to be with them. They weren't shocked to hear the sound of the Lord. They did hide from God after they sinned against Him, but the regular time that they were going to have with Him was no surprise to them. In fact, Adam not being present made God ask the question in verse 9, *"Where are you?"*

Adam and Eve didn't know they were naked before they had sinned. And of course, they did certainly die spiritually. Ephesians 2:1 says we were dead in trespasses and sins, which is speaking of a spiritual death. Though they didn't die physically, at least not right then (930 years later, see Gen. 5:5), they immediately died spiritually. The moment sin entered the world, death took the life out of humanity and began its cycle of death and destruction both spiritually and physically. I would also suggest that the Spirit of God, who had covered them, left them when they trespassed; and therefore they noticed their nakedness and their shame. Their eyes were immediately opened to a new set of fleshly desires that were corrupt.

Robert S. McGee, in his book *The Search for Significance,* concludes, "One of the tragic implications of this event is that man lost his secure status with God and began to struggle with feelings of arrogance, inadequacy, and despair, valuing the opinions of others more than the truth of God."[8]

FLIPPED UPSIDE DOWN

When God is connected to our spirit, we submit to His leadership and allow Him to direct our soul (our mind, will, and emotions) and command our physical bodies (with our five senses). This is how we were originally created and were supposed to continue to live, from the inside out. But when sin entered the world, things were flipped upside down and people began living from the *outside in,* which explains why Adam and Eve knew they were naked. From this point on, Adam and all humankind were then led by their flesh and the natural impulses of the physical body, which in turn affects the soul. So what was once alive before Adam and Eve sinned, was now dead due to sin. A spirit outside of the life of God, not following the Spirit of God is dead.

THREE-PART BEING

Now may the God of peace Himself sanctify you completely; and may your whole spirit, soul, and body be preserved blameless at the coming of our Lord Jesus Christ (1 Thessalonians 5:23).

For one year, when my wife and I first entered into ministry, we lived with my in-laws, Mark and Karen Anderson. Many evenings, Mark taught me biblical truths that imparted so much life into me in a way that Bible university never did, for which I am eternally grateful. One night Mark showed me First Thessalonians 5:23, and it struck me and showed me the way we were fashioned by God, which sent me on a journey.

Through the years I have done my own study and many others have also influenced my thoughts on this. Let's start with the word that sticks out to me first, the word "sanctify," which simply means to be "set apart for God's exclusive use or consecrated unto Him."[9] There are at least three different ways this term is used in the New Testament.

> First, there is *positional* sanctification. This is when you believed in Christ as your Savior and Lord, you were instantaneously, set apart for God (Heb. 10:10). Secondly, there is *progressive* sanctification. This refers to your daily growth in holiness (2 Cor. 7:1). Thirdly, there is *perfective* sanctification. This takes place when you see Christ and become eternally like Him (1 John 3:2). It is this last meaning of sanctification that Paul has in mind here. He prays that God will "entirely" sanctify the Thessalonians. He prays that their entire person: body, soul and spirit be preserved until the coming of Jesus. The word translated "preserved" (*tereo*) is a word that typically means, "*To watch over, keep.*" God Himself will ensure your salvation and Christian growth. It is God who does this work!"[10]

When someone gives his or her life to Jesus Christ, the person's spirit is born again.

> The believer's born-again (John 3:3) spirit is complete in every way. But Paul made it very clear in this verse that it is God's will for our entire person to be sanctified. Our soul and body will not experience the same degree of sanctification as our spirit until we are with the Lord. We can be *blameless* but not sinless (1 Cor. 1:8).

> At the new birth our dead spirit is made alive unto God. The Christian is completely new in his spirit. The rest of the Christian life is bringing the body and the soul under the control

of this born-again spirit through the renewing of the mind (Rom. 12:2).[11]

This is confirmed in Hebrews 10. Let's look at it.

For by one offering [sacrifice] *He* [Jesus] *has perfected forever those who are being sanctified* (Hebrews 10:14).

To describe the sacrifice of Jesus, the writer uses the perfect tense: He has *perfected*. It is final and complete. Nothing needs to be added or taken away from it. Describing the work of *sanctification*, on the other hand, the writer uses a progressive tense: they are *being sanctified*. Becoming holy is a stage-by-stage continuance of what has already been made available to us by the sacrifice of Jesus. The Holy Spirit is our helper in this process.[12]

God is dealing with our three-part being. He saved our spirit; and as we set our heart on obedience to the Lord, our soul is being renewed day by day, mainly through the Word of God and fellowship with the Spirit of God. Although our physical body will disintegrate, it needs to come under the control of the new self (spirit) and the renewed mind.

I just love seeing how God made us in His image to reflect His three-part being. In the same way the Trinity is three yet one, humans have three parts as well. We see entwined throughout the Bible how God used the number three in many ways, which represents divine fullness and completeness. Let's see how He did that with the tabernacle of Moses.

MOSES' TABERNACLE—A PROPHETIC PICTURE

And let them make Me a sanctuary, that I may dwell among them. According to all that I show you, that is, the pattern of the tabernacle and the pattern of all its furnishings, just so you shall make it (Exodus 25:8-9).

From the very beginning, God desired to dwell with humankind and made every way possible to dwell among us in intimacy. Because sin separated us from Him, He wanted to make a way to have us near Him; or better yet, He wanted to be near us. As a result, He instructed Moses to make a tabernacle for humankind to worship and come to Him and commune with Him. The tabernacle of Moses is a prophetic picture of how God created us for two purposes: for communion and worship.

In the tabernacle there was the outer court, the inner court, and the Holy of Holies (see Exod. 35-40). In a later chapter I will explain a bit further the intimacy with God that this represents. This is important to acknowledge because everything is layered in threes. God is a triune God. We are three-part beings, and Moses' tabernacle had three tiers to its layout. What the tabernacle once was, we now exemplify in our very physical bodies today, in New Testament context.

Or do you not know that your body is the temple of the Holy Spirit who is in you, whom you have from God, and you are not your own? (1 Corinthians 6:19)

You and I are tri-part beings. You are a spirit being. You possess a soul (mind, will, and emotions) and you live in a body (with its five senses: taste, see, hear, touch, and smell). You're an eternal spirit who lives in a body. The tabernacle of Moses is no longer needed because you and I are now the tabernacle. This is shown in our makeup of spirit, soul, and body. Let me explain.

- The outer court represents the human body. This is the part that you see, taste, touch, hear, and smell. It's the physical part of you that can be seen in the mirror. If you were to be talking to me, you would see my face, my appearance, but that's not who I really am.

- Next is the inner court that represents the soul of a person. This includes the mind, will, emotion, intellect, and memory. This is the mental and emotional part of the human makeup. I would also include your conscience as a part of your soul. Your inner part can't be seen but it can be felt. Most people think this is the core of who they are, but that is not true. The Word says it much differently, defining your spirit self as the core of who you are.

- Finally you have the Holy of Holies, which is the human spirit or the innermost part of your being. This is what lives for eternity. Your flesh will eventually die and turn into ground or dirt; but the human spirit lives forever—whether in hell or in heaven, it will live for eternity. This is where the Holy Spirit comes to reside in us when we give over our lives to Him. He comes to give us new life and we are therefore reborn and alive in Christ. *"That which is born of the flesh is flesh, and that which is born of the Spirit is spirit"* (John 3:6). This innermost part of who you are is the center, the core of your being. It can't be seen or felt, but this is the real you. Your spirit is your life-giving part.

Andrew Wommack compels us to get hold of the truth of our human makeup. "Understanding the spirit, soul and body unlocks the spirit realm so you can experience who you are and what you have in Christ."[13]

WHICH PART LEADS WHAT?

It is important to consider how we are created, but more importantly how we are meant to live, from the inside out.

So let me ask you to consider a question to honestly evaluate. Which part of your three-part being leads your life? Does your physical body, with its five senses? Is your soul, with the constant barrage of thoughts that come to your mind? Or how about your emotions, happy or sad, depressed or at peace? What about your spirit self who is in relationship with your Creator God living inside you? Which part of your being is leading your life?

My father-in-law, Mark, shared an example with me years ago, and I have taken it and made it my own. I have now shared this example with many people worldwide. When speaking, I like to invite three people on stage with me to show them an example that they can understand.

I first ask for the biggest, strongest man in the room to come to the front. Then I invite a medium-size person to stand next to him. I end by asking the smallest, skinniest person there to join us up front.

I share the example showing that the biggest and strongest person is going to represent the flesh, or the physical body. This is our "outer court," which the majority of the time we let lead our lives.

Second, the medium-size person or the "inner court" represents the soul, led through our thoughts, emotions, and will. Many people are actually led more by their emotions and thoughts than anything else; but for the sake of the example, we will leave it at number two.

Finally, the small, skinny person represents the spirit self, which is usually not leading anything, but being dragged along succumbing to all our soulish and physical desires. This person, who represents most of our starved spirit selves, is not strong enough and is not being fed enough to withstand the soul and flesh.

This, my friend, is what I call living from the outside. This is contrary to how we were created and is definitely not the best that God has to offer. We were meant to flip these guys around and have the strongest be our spirit self, letting the Holy Spirit within us strengthen us as we feed ourselves a rich diet of the Word of God and communion with Him.

Before I close this thought, I want you to know that neither your physical body nor your soul is bad and should not be viewed negatively. In fact it is very good. God made you perfect and called it "good." Neither your physical body nor your soul should be leading your life, however; you are meant to live from the inside out, by your spirit connected to the very nature of God.

How it all Works Together

So let's clarify how your three-part being works together.

> When your soul agrees with your spirit, the life of God in you will manifest itself in your physical body. You'll experience healing, deliverance, anointing, victory, power, joy and prosperity—on and on it goes.

> Since most Christians don't have a working knowledge of spirit, soul, and body, they're dominated by what they can see, taste, hear, smell, and feel instead of by God's Word. The flow of life within stays turned off because they don't believe anything they can't see. Neither do they understand the change that happened in their born-again spirits, nor are they fully aware of who they are in Christ. To them, something's just not real if it can't be perceived through their five senses. Attempting to be "honest," they search their physical, emotional, and mental realms for God's power. If they can't perceive it, then they must not have it.[14]

> *His divine power has given us everything we need for a godly life through our knowledge of him who called us by his own glory and goodness. Through these he has given us his very*

great and precious promises, so that through them you may participate in the divine nature, having escaped the corruption in the world caused by evil desires (2 Peter 1:3-4 NIV).

What an incredible truth: we have everything we need for life and godliness. The Christian walk is rewarded with everything we need on the front end and receiving, contending, discovering, and experiencing God's divine nature for the rest of our lives, even in the age to come. "The rest of your Christian life should be spent learning how to manifest in the physical realm what's already in your born-again spirit."[15]

INSIDE-OUT LIVING

The way we are supposed to live is to build or strengthen our spirit self and have this part lead our lives. Then we are to renew our mind by washing it through the water of the Word of God (see Rom. 12:2 and Eph. 5:26), so that we come into agreement with who God is and who we are in Christ. Allowing our physical bodies to follow suit.

John the Baptist is a perfect example of living with a strong spirit and being led by his spirit.

So the child grew and became strong in spirit, and was in the deserts till the day of his manifestation to Israel (Luke 1:80).

This is the model for us to follow. If John the Baptist became strong in spirit, so can we. Later on in other chapters, I will expound on how to strengthen and develop the interior life of the believer and experience pleasure with God. Inside-out living requires a transforming of your soul and is strengthening of your spirit and a determination to walk out your life in agreement with His purposes and who God says you are.

Chapter 3

DIVINE PLEASURE

If I find in myself a desire which no experience
in this world can satisfy, the most probable
explanation is that I was made for another world.
—C.S. LEWIS, *A Mind Awake*

Communion with the indwelling God that results in us living a vibrant life from the inside out is one of the simplest things to do, yet is the hardest to sustain as a true reality. Once we get a glimpse of this reality and how God's grace is there to empower us, we begin to see the endless possibilities of a life alive in God. We taste the divine pleasure that impacts our heart that keeps us coming back for more.

Many Christians began their Christian walk communing with God, but for various reasons, after some time, we negated this reality and resigned ourselves to living our lives like He is not even there. In the midst of going through the motions of daily life, we so often forget that He's closer than our breath.

The question is why? Why don't we commune with the God who made every way possible for us to live a vibrant life? The God who made a way for us to access not just His heavenly, eternal throne, but most importantly His heart? The fact remains that so much of our lives we simply don't live out this reality of close relationship with God.

We can expand on these thoughts by asking ourselves some more questions. If God is so good, why don't we seek Him out? If He's so amazing, why do we rarely encounter His amazing love? If He's so beautiful, why do we hardly look to see Him? If His Word is alive, why do we hardly encounter the *life* of the Word and the man Jesus between the lines of the Bible? If His sheep hear His voice, why do we so rarely hear it? (See John 10:27.)

These unanswered questions and others reveal to us the issue that lies behind our lack of pursuing God's heart and the lack of our knowledge of Him.

WRONG VIEW OF GOD

I believe that we rarely if ever commune with the God living inside us because of our *wrong view of God*. For many of us, much of our view of God is that of a mostly angry, disappointed, judgmental God who wants our money, our time, and our forced obedience. Some feel like they can never make God happy; and on top of that they feel gnawing guilt that results in half-hearted attempts at having a relationship with Him. Others think because God paid such a high price, they should at least attempt to serve Him. These feelings of obligation result in settling for giving a little money and a little time and service. We have head knowledge of this man named Jesus who gave His life for us, while rarely, if ever, do we encounter Jesus Himself. We neglect to really see and experience the very reason, passion, and desire behind what He did and why He did it. You see, for so many of us, we have a distorted view of who God really is.

We need a right view of God to live life the way He intended us to live and to have hearts that experience the pleasure above all pleasures—intimately knowing God. There is a direct correlation between how we view God, and how we view ourselves. If we view God as a harsh, disappointed, angry taskmaster, we will always feel like we are falling short. We will in turn view our own lives with discouragement and condemnation while feeling like a continued failure in trying to meet His standard. When we have a wrong view of God, we can have a wrong view of ourselves, leading to a wrong view of prayer, holiness, and a wrong view of our lives. When we attempt to do the right thing and fall short, our wrong view of God affects our thinking and we perceive things like, "God is mad and disappointed with me, and I'm just a hypocrite anyway, so why try?"

When we have a distorted view of God, we fail to see the truth of who He really is and what He thinks and feels for us. We can neglect to see the infinite worth and value we and others have in God's sight. Wrong thinking of God is detrimental and affects every area of our lives; we end up just going through the motions. We come to the conclusion that we need to pay the price and attend boring Christian meetings. Yet we fail to see that the prayer meetings are only boring because we really are not experiencing God or feeling the exhilarating pleasure of knowing Him. We end up not feeling His touch because we think He is completely different from who He really is.

DETERMINING OUR VIEW THROUGH OTHERS

Another way to see the areas in which we have a wrong view of God is to look at how we treat others. The way you feel Father God treats you is how you will treat others. If you treat people harshly, you probably think God treats you in the same manner. If you have a hard time forgiving, you may not feel you are forgiven. If you are critical of others, tearing them down, you may feel God does this with you. These are just a few examples of ways you may have a distorted view of God.

On the flip side however, if you are helpful, you probably think that God is helpful. If you are compassionate and merciful, then more than likely you see God rightly in those areas. If you are kind and tender toward others, you feel God is this way with you. Let me expand this through looking at a Scripture:

You shall love your neighbor as yourself (Mark 12:31).

This is a radical way to live our lives in loving people. This exposes how we view ourselves and how we view God along with how we love people. You'll notice in this passage, God doesn't want you to love people as you love Him. He is commanding you to love people as you love yourself because you're supposed to love yourself as you love God. He is the Source; and as you love yourself, you are to love people. Everyone loves themselves and has a desire to be happy. That is how we are to love people, out of the abundance of self-love.

> "As you love yourself, so love your neighbor." Which means: As you long for food when you are hungry, so long to feed your neighbor when he is hungry. As you long for nice clothes for yourself, so long for nice clothes for your neighbor. As you work for a comfortable place to live, so desire a comfortable place to live for your neighbor. As you seek to be safe and secure from calamity and violence, so seek comfort and security for your neighbor. As you seek friends for yourself, so be a friend to your neighbor. As you want your life to count and be significant, so desire that same significance for your neighbor."[1]

Self-love is what everyone already knows. No one has to be taught this; it's naturally already in every human being. God calls us to love our neighbor out of this self-love, which is really based on how we view God. If we view God correctly and love Him rightly, we will love ourselves better which will overflow into loving people.

If we have a right view of God knowing that as His children His heart is tender and compassionate toward us, we will be filled with confidence in His love and affection toward us. When we are awakened to His passion and set our hearts to obey and love Him, He is pleased with our reach toward Him no matter how weak it may be.

Therefore, one of the biggest keys for communion with God is to view God rightly. So much hinges on this. If we view God correctly, we will go near Him, instead of run away from Him.

Satan, our enemy, lives to distort our view of God. He is constantly accusing Him to our heart and skewing our view of Him, so we would run away from Him instead of to Him. That is why in Hebrews 4:16 God calls us to *"come boldly to the throne of grace."* I believe this is the greatest key to intimacy with God.

That is why I have devoted the next few chapters to realigning our view of God, the Trinity, and how He views us in response. If we can get hold of this, I believe we will have a new perspective that will deepen our communion with God.

BEHOLDING HIS GLORY

When our hearts are touched with even a taste of His great love for us, we begin the process of being changed from the inside. In the next chapter, I write about the "Beholding Becoming" principle, which is: as we behold His glory we are changed from glory to glory, being transformed into His likeness more each day (see 2 Cor. 3:18), all the while our hearts are being exhilarated in Him. Our focus is to behold His glory. With this focus, sin, pain, and the cares of this world pale in comparison to the incomparable riches of knowing God. The favor and passion the Lord has for us is unfathomable in our minds. What is available in and through God is really an injustice. We do not deserve such radical forgiveness, love, and acceptance.

I encourage you to begin to search out the emotions of God in the Bible and watch as truth of who God is transforms you. To the degree that we understand God rightly, or better said, the degree we really behold Him for who He is, we will be transformed in how we see ourselves and how we love others. We will be unstoppable lovers of God, full of confidence with the ability to "throw off the sin that so easily entangles us" (see Heb. 12:1). Without a doubt, what we need is a paradigm shift of our view of God. This is one of the most important aspects of living a life of intimacy and enjoying God from the inside!

BEYOND COMPREHENSION

But as it is written: "Eye has not seen, nor ear heard, nor have entered into the heart of man the things which God has prepared for those who love Him" (1 Corinthians 2:9).

The knowledge of God is astounding; His passion for us is so great, and what He has prepared for us is beyond our wildest dreams and imaginations—all because of who God is (1 Cor. 2:9). As I search out the truths of who God really is, I am blown away by the new facets of God that I am continually discovering. What fascinates me is that God is so infinite that if we were to grab one attribute of who God is, such as mercy, the vastness of that one attribute will take us on a search for all of eternity and still never reach the end of it. If we were to search out the mercy of God and study His mercy for the next billion years, we would never reach the end of knowing the full infinite wonder of how merciful God is.

This majestic thought propels me to seek God out, knowing that I will never be bored, but perpetually exhilarated in the awesome wonder of God. I can confidently say, I have barely scratched the surface of knowing who God is. That thought alone exhilarates me with the excitement of the endless possibilities and mysteries that are found for those who press into knowing and searching Him out! Come join me!

RIGHT VIEW OF GOD

The chief end of man is to glorify God and enjoy Him forever. —JOHN PIPER

I am a man who is constantly looking for the next big thrill. I am looking for constant pleasure and happiness everywhere. That may sound strange, but it is very likely that you are too. We humans were designed by God Himself to look for and experience pleasure. John Piper reveals, "it is not a bad thing to desire our own good, in fact, the great problem of human beings is that they are far too easily pleased. They don't seek pleasure with nearly the resolve and passion that they should. And so they settle for mud pies of appetite instead of infinite delight."[2]

God designed us to pursue pleasure so that it would lead us to Him: the Author of pleasure. It is very important that as I begin to talk about finding and experiencing pleasure, true pleasure in God, that we realize that no earthly pleasures will ever satisfy. We are told this, but few of us actually believe it. I dare you to taste of Him, and in doing so you will get a small glimpse of what you were created for.

During far too much of my life, I looked for pleasure in the wrong places that never satisfied me. I never realized I was eating mud pies instead of feasting at God's banqueting table. God was that longing and that yearning. The feeling when I finally encountered God was entirely fascinating and exhilarating; feelings of divine pleasure finally began to make sense and only made me come back for more. I can easily and unashamedly say that I am a pleasure seeker; seeking the pleasures of my God. I now know that my sights were not set high enough in my pursuit of pleasure. My mistake was not in wanting to experience pleasure or happiness but that it was far too weak of a desire!

SEEKING HAPPINESS

There are many natural, God-given pleasures, which are healthy and not sinful, that God has given me to enjoy, such as loving my wife, enjoying my kids, friendships with others, eating delicious food, and more. But even these earthly pleasures God has given us do not compare with the euphoric pleasure of experiencing and knowing God intimately.

A good explanation that brings clarity to our desire to seek happiness and pleasure is written by Blaise Pascal:

> All men seek happiness. This is without exception. Whatever different means they employ, they all tend to this end. The cause of some going to war, and of others avoiding it, is the same desire in both, attended with different views. The will never takes the least step but to this object. This is the motive of every action of every man, even of those who hang themselves.[3]

Let me add to this point what Jonathan Edwards expressed, "The soul of every man necessarily craves happiness, this is a universal appetite of human nature, that is alike in the good and the bad.[4]

Seeking pleasure in itself is not bad, as I had thought for so long; it is seeking it outside of God that it becomes counterfeit and less fulfilling. This idea that all pleasure is wrong is not something really verbalized in the Church, but rather an underlying subtle belief that is felt, yet unspoken.

HAPPINESS VERSUS HUMANISM

I had thought that seeking my own happiness was not something godly or beneficial. After all, the doctrine of humanism, which promotes self-oriented worship and self-satisfaction, was something I was trying to avoid. I didn't see that seeking the true and superior pleasure of loving God was the purpose and key to my life.

Humanism, which is only focused on self and self-gratification, has crept into the Church with crippling effects. The self-absorbed aren't interested in loving our neighbor, preaching the Gospel, financial giving, missions, serving, and much more. How often we hear that the best way to live is to "do whatever makes you happy." The way we live our lives much of the time mirrors our belief in this selfish system. Humanism, where humankind is god, has been joined together with secularism, which is *the throwing off all restraint of disciplines, holiness and worst of all, moral absolutes.*

When you combine secularism and humanism to make secular humanism, you have the description of the society in which we live today. At its core, secular humanism focuses solely on tolerance-driven, counterfeit, pleasure-seeking fulfillment of every sensual, sexual, lust-filled, pride-filled, self-indulgent appetite, no matter how big or small it is. The goal is having as much as you want, when you want; and if anyone tells you otherwise, they are outdated, religious, intolerant, or bigots. The Church has adopted this mindset in so many ways that the Church even creates sermons and doctrines to suit our itching ears.

I hold firmly to combatting this way of life with every means possible and giving my life up to the lordship of Jesus Christ. My purpose in saying all of this to you is not to rant on about our culture, but to expose the prevalence of this mindset that is in direct contrast to God's intended life for us. A life steeped with secular humanism is an inferior way of living, and is not the same as seeking pleasure through loving God and being fascinated by who He is. After all, I want to be known as a hungry man, seeking the knowledge of God, and pleasing Him in every way possible, experiencing as much pleasure as I can have in Him. This pursuit of true pleasure leads me to being the most satisfied and yet unsatisfied man, all at the same time!

ENJOYING GOD IS NOT WRONG

A side note: there are some cultures, especially in years past that viewed all pleasure as evil. These attitudes have remained to some degree and have been passed down even into our Christian mindsets. There is a belief that if something is enjoyable, it should be viewed with suspicion and disdain. How could something that is godly be enjoyable at the same time? This is from where much of the confusion has come. J.I. Packer states, "The emotional side of knowing God is often played down these days, for fear of encouraging maudlin self-absorption."[5]

Unfortunately, enjoying God is foreign to many of us and some even feel it is wrong "because," they reason, "if it is too pleasurable it must be wrong." When children, for example, are enjoying themselves and we are not enjoying ourselves like they are, we can either join in the fun or we can get grumpy and stop all the happiness. Let's be a people who keep our childlikeness and dive into knowing Him. I am not talking about casting off moral or emotional restraints; I am talking about enjoying the nature of God, which is the highest form of pleasure and experience.

GOD—AUTHOR OF PLEASURE

You will show me the path of life; in Your presence is fullness of joy; at Your right hand are pleasures forevermore (Psalm 16:11).

True happiness and pleasure aren't things that God gives by delivering it to us on a plate; we must find it in Him. God is the Author of pleasure. Psalm 16:11 reveals for us that He has infinite pleasure forever. He is the Creator and the Source of pleasure. He is the all-satisfying object of pleasure and satisfaction.

The part that really awakens something in me is in the second portion of this verse, *"in Your presence is fullness of joy"*. What a statement!

This was one of the secrets of King David's life—his aim to know what moved God's heart. This constant "discovering" of God caused David to have great joy, or better yet, know God as joy. There are many pleasures in life that God has given us to enjoy; but, the pleasure of God Himself is the ultimate pleasure, for He is the Author of it. In Psalm 16:11, David in essence is saying, "You're a God of gladness; you're overflowing with gladness." That's why I believe David was a man after God's heart; he experienced a taste of God, His heart and His goodness, and David was in an all-out hunt for this transcendent pleasure again and again—he was a man *after* God's heart.

I appreciate what Sam Storms asks us to consider, "Think about what David is saying. God is offering us a joy that infinitely transcends all other joys combined in the power and potential to satisfy, thrill, fill and fulfill. He is talking about spiritual ecstasy, incomparable ecstasy, unparalleled ecstasy, and unfathomable ecstasy. And it is all to be found in only one place: in God's presence, at His right hand."[6]

DELIGHT IN THE LORD

In Christianity today, we often have a distorted view that pleasure is wrong and bad, and because we enjoy something it must be wrong. So we correlate that relating to God should not be enjoyable. We've believed the lie that *sin is exciting and God is boring* and we need to *pay the price to be with God*. But I will say, not only should we enjoy God, but also we are commanded to delight ourselves in the Lord (see Ps. 37:4). This is a holy invitation. Once you taste of the Lord, He knows you will keep coming back for more of Him. "I do not say that loving God is good because it brings joy. I say that God commands that we find joy in loving God."[7]

> *Delight yourself also in the Lord, and He shall give you the desires of your heart* (Psalm 37:4).

Enjoying God and finding pleasure in Him is the foundation to intimacy, communion, and relationship with God; and it is unbiblical to believe anything else. God is the Author of pleasure. Enjoying God produces a worship of Him that just spills out of us. All true pleasure originates in God, and the devil only counterfeits it. God created pleasures: physical pleasures, mental pleasures, emotional pleasures, and spiritual ones. But the most profound and greatest pleasures are spiritual in nature. The greatest pleasures available to the human spirit are when God reveals God to us. There is nothing like when the Holy Spirit reveals God's emotions, His beauty, and His lovingkindness—the exhilaration that comes to our spirit is beyond words.

Sam Storms, in his book *Pleasures Evermore,* examines the way David described this thirst and longing that is only satisfied in God. He compared his yearning for God with the vivid imagery of a deer in a desert land, panting for life-giving water: 'As the deer pants for the water brooks, so my soul pants for thee, O God. My soul thirsts for God, for the living God' (see Ps. 42:1-2). The focus in this word-picture is not the deer, but the water. It is on the cool, refreshing, sustaining properties of the desert stream that all eyes are fixed. The deer brings nothing to the brooks but its desperation and its thirst. This is how we must come to God."[8]

FIRST-TIME ENCOUNTERS OF REAL PLEASURE

One of the first times I encountered the enjoyment of God was when I was 15 years old. I had just returned from church with my family and immediately I went directly to watch the football game on TV with my dad. While eating some potato chips, I felt like I heard a small voice, which was mixed with an urge to go and speak with God. I felt the nudge and the call to go and spend time with God. I passed it off as no big deal. But I kept hearing these recurring words, "Come and talk with Me, come and be with Me," over and over. These words were full of emotion; I could feel them. I couldn't overlook them as some passing voice, like a phone call I didn't want to answer at that moment but could call back later. I knew it was God and I knew He was talking to me and inviting me to speak to Him and be with Him. The food, the game, the company, was nothing compared to how I felt inside. I felt like I was going to burst with tears, happiness, and great excitement, all at the same time. I was getting ready to embark on the biggest thrill of my life.

The words just kept hitting my heart, "Come and talk with Me, come be with Me!" I had to answer Him. So like a volcano, I erupted in response. I shot up out of my chair, threw my chips to the floor, and ran as if there was an emergency. I was running into the arms of my Father, and I was running to Jesus and the Holy Spirit all at the same time. I ran to my room, threw myself to the floor and said, "Here I am. I love You, Jesus." That day I encountered the most satisfying pleasure of communing with God that I have ever had. Jesus became more than just God in the third heaven; He became real to me on the inside. His voice was like refreshing waves; He was so real, so near.

This encounter led me on a journey for the next several months of reading the Bible for long hours, speaking to Him about what I read, asking questions, and talking with Him for hours. I sang to Him, I cried with Him, not tears of sadness, but tears of overflowing joy. This was one of the greatest seasons of my life; I have continued to come back for more ever since. I encountered the God of pleasure!

My Son and the Man between the Lines

My 11-year-old son, Gabriel, has been encountering the God-Man Jesus between the lines of the Bible. Many people think it's a book to read for intellectual information only. Oh, beloved it's so much more than that.

For the word of God is living and powerful, and sharper than any two-edged sword, piercing even to the division of soul and spirit, and of joints and marrow, and is a discerner of the thoughts and intents of the heart (Hebrews 4:12).

Gabriel decided earlier this year to read the Bible all the way through, cover to cover. Christelle and I didn't know if it would last or what would really happen. More than anything we were just happy that he entered into this decision on his own. No matter how many days the decision lasted, it was pretty cool to see him even desire this.

What happened to him was amazing! He developed feelings of longing and desire for continual encounter through the Word of God. We started seeing that he would spend long hours reading more than ever before. Anytime we would study as a family, he wanted us to read where he was. His fun times were spent reading and more reading. One Saturday morning while I talked to my kids about the pleasures of enjoying and encountering God, he came to us afterward and said that's exactly how he felt when he read the Bible. Gabriel continued to say:

> I love reading the Bible when I get on the bus in the morning, on my way to school. I read the whole time, and when I'm at school I can't wait to get on the bus and read the Bible again. Then I go home and I can't wait to read it some more. I try to get other people reading the Bible with me so they can feel what I'm feeling.
>
> Reading the Bible gives me what I want. Watching TV doesn't give me what I want, the Bible does. Praying also does. I get to spend time with the greatest Person who ever walked this earth. I get to spend time with the King of kings. That's what reading the Bible makes me feel.

This newfound passion did not go unnoticed at Gabriel's school as well. I received an email from his teacher, Mrs. Joyce Stigter. She wrote:

We always do ARP tests in Grade 5. This entails choosing a designated ARP book…reading it and then taking a computer-generated comprehension test…When I reviewed Gabriel's ARP results for the month of May with him, he communicated to me that he didn't really want to read any other book than the Bible. I was surprised and…felt it was important to honor his desire to just read the Bible and I told him on Thursday that I would make my own ARP tests for three of the books of the Bible that he has already read. He told me that he wanted to be tested on Deuteronomy, Joshua and Judges…I also noticed recently that a couple of other students in the class are wanting to read through the whole Bible as well, something that Gabriel has inspired them to do.

Gabriel is not simply reading a book, he pulls out phrases and concepts that he reads and talks to God about them. He told us that if he didn't understand something he was reading, he would just ask the Holy Spirit about it, and the Holy Spirit would explain it to him. Gabriel is encountering God while he reads the Bible. He is experiencing what he was always meant to experience, intimacy with his Creator. These are superior pleasures!

THE CLOSER TO THE THRONE, THE HAPPIER WE BECOME

There is great pleasure found in reading and talking to God about the Bible. One of my favorite pleasures is when revelation touches me as I read the Bible and I come alive inside. I encounter the man Jesus and revelation allows me to understand what is being said as it is imparted to me.

I want you to think for a minute about the throne of God as described in Revelation chapter 4. If you were to be transported by the

Holy Spirit to the throne of God right now, you would be shocked! You would have a combination of overwhelming terror of the exhilaration of God's majesty and an overflowing exuberance, joy, and happiness simultaneously. You would feel so many varied emotions that you would be saying, "More, I want more! No, I can't handle anymore! It's too much! Never enough! God, You're too much, but I can't handle it! I want more, just give me more! Oh, get me out of here! It feels so good! Oh, it's so horrifying!" It's simply too intense for our earthly understanding. This picture of extreme pleasure brings home the Scripture in Psalm 16:11 that at His right hand is fullness of joy and pleasures forevermore.

> We were made to enjoy Him. Our minds were shaped and fashioned to think about God, to reflect and meditate on His majesty and beauty and to experience the intellectual thrill of theological discovery. Our emotions were made to feel His power, love and longing for us. Our wills were made to choose His will and ways; our spirits were formed to experience the ecstasy of communion with Him; our bodies were fashioned to be the temple where He Himself would delight to dwell![9]

LACK OF FASCINATION

Since we were made to enjoy God to the fullest and to be fascinated by Him, one of the biggest challenges we face is boredom. "Boredom is the breeding ground for wickedness. Bored people are easy targets of the flesh and the Devil."[10] Let me give you an example.

My friend Aaron Melanson is a world-renowned break-dancer and a lover of Jesus. He takes his break-dancing skills around the world and shares his testimony, inviting people to make a decision to follow Christ.

Before Aaron gave his life to Jesus, he was in the party scene, break-dancing in raves and clubs. He took various forms of drugs and alcohol.

He would even deal drugs to get his drugs covered for the night. One specific drug that he would take and sell was the drug called ecstasy.

What Is Ecstasy?

Ecstasy is a common name for a drug that is very popular among young adults. It's an illegal drug that can be very damaging to your body and can even lead to death.

Dr. Foster Olive says that ecstasy is a hallucinogen that falsely "intensifies physical sensations and perceptions and produces heightened self-esteem and sociability along with profound feelings of euphoria, love and empathy."[11] Ecstasy distorts the perception of normal objects and heightens the senses.

Aaron explained why he would use the drug, "I would take ecstasy to escape something. I didn't know what I was escaping, but without it I felt trapped. I would get into tunnel vision of just enjoying the moment and feeling really, really good. It was a false pleasure I could experience in that moment. It was a euphoric feeling all night long." He would feel like this at least until the drug wore off.

Taking this drug and many other drugs like it is a far cry from real pleasure. It leaves people with major consequences and regrets, even causing death. Dr. Foster Olive adds, "It does not just have potent effects on the brain—it acts in numerous other symptoms in the body, and many of the effects can be harmful or fatal."[12] When the drug wears off it leaves you depressed and eventually sucks dry the chemicals in your body that produce enjoyment. The side effects of a drug like this range from high blood pressure, fevers, depression, anger and anxiety, often resulting in death.

The reason I shared all of this was to let you see how far people will go to experience pleasure. Millions of people get high on ecstasy, abuse alcohol and various other substances to escape and feel some pleasure even if it is false and short-lived. People have such a desire for pleasure that they think no cost and no consequence is too great to feel it, even if it is counterfeit and short-term.

A BORED KING

Let me also show you an example of the effects of boredom from the life of David. As you read this, pay close attention to where David was, as well as the specific times of day.

> *It happened in the spring of the year, at the time when kings go out to battle, that David sent Joab and his servants with him, and all Israel; and they destroyed the people of Ammon and besieged Rabbah. But David remained at Jerusalem. Then it happened one evening that David arose from his bed and walked on the roof of the king's house. And from the roof he saw a woman bathing, and the woman was very beautiful to behold* (2 Samuel 11:1-2).

David is shown here to be bored, which led him to be distracted, which led to falling into sin. God gives some revealing details in this portion of Scripture to help us understand how David got into this mess in the first place.

When kings go out to battle in the springtime, David was not there. This was the beginning of the chain of events. If David had been at battle, the rightful place for him as king, none of the options to make the wrong decision would have been placed in front of him.

Another important part to see is that David rose from his bed in the evening time. In today's terms, David was "chilling and vegging out," when he was supposed to be fighting a war. He lost his focus, he became lazy, and his boredom led him straight into sin.

Our hearts were made to be fascinated and enraptured by the beauty of God; and if we let Him, He will fill our gnawing longing for pleasure. He is what we are looking for. I encourage you, if you are not enjoying

God, begin to do so now. You may be saying, "I want to, but how?" I will describe practical ways to enjoy God in later chapters of this book, but know that this enjoyment is not out of reach for any one of you. God does not lack a single thing, and once you taste of Him, you will keep coming back for more and more. God loves to fill us, thrill us, and bring us into His fulfillment.

In his book *The Seven Longings of the Human Heart,* Mike Bickle explains,

> Tragically, the inferior pleasures of sin have the potential to dominate our lives if they are the only pleasures we experience. If someone has not experienced God, or has very little knowledge of who He is, the inferior pleasure of sin seems, as worthy fulfillment, rather than the hollow counterfeit we know it to be. Many Christians focus only on resisting the inferior pleasures Satan offers. They look at their sin and promise God, "I'll never, ever, ever do that again!" They make promises they can't keep and go through religious incantations as they seek to be set free. Still, in the back of their minds they're remembering that their sin was pleasurable.[13]
>
> God desires to awe us with the pleasures available only in relationship with Him. He taps us on the shoulder and whispers, "Turn around! Look at the superior pleasures of the beauty of My Son, the greatness of who you are in God— My chosen partner who will rule and reign with me forever and ever!" It is when we fix our eyes on these things, on the greater pleasure of God, that something happens in our hearts.[14]

How do we overcome lesser pleasures? The answer is with our enjoyment of God! "We minimize our delight in the pleasures of the flesh by maximizing our delight in the pleasures of our Creator. Oh, taste and see that the Lord is good!"[15]

In Summary

Throughout this chapter, I unpacked many aspects of who God is and what can be found in Him when we view Him rightly. I wrote this in hopes that it would inspire and propel you into deep communion with God. In fact, there is no other meaning and purpose in life that surpasses knowing God and communing with Him; it's why you were created. He takes great pleasure in being with you!

> *You are worthy, O Lord, to receive glory and honor and power; for you created all things, and by your will* [pleasure] *they exist and were created* (Revelation 4:11).

God created us for His divine pleasure. That is why we exist, that is why we were created, and that is our earthly and eternal purpose. In closing, A.W. Tozer helps to summarize it like this,

> God made man to be like Him so that man could give more pleasure to God than all the other creatures. Only in man, as created by God, can God admire Himself. Man is the reflection of the glory of God, which was the purpose and intention of God originally. Man's supreme function through all eternity is to reflect God's highest glory, and that God might look into the mirror called man and see His own glory shining there. Through man, God could reflect His glory to all creation.[16]

An Invitation

This is an invitation that God is extending to you. I pray that you would allow the following verse in Psalm 27 to be a personal invitation to you as God invites you to fellowship with Him.

My heart has heard you say, "Come and talk with me." And my heart responds, "Lord, I am coming" (Psalm 27:8 NLT).

Once you truly taste the authenticity of His love, you will come back again and again and again. His voice is calling you into His heart and it will only increase as you answer it, in the midst of real life and work! God is calling you to go and speak with Him, tell Him what is on your heart, listen to Him and wait on Him. He is after your heart—and deep down you're after His heart too!

As our view of God changes, we are changed; and not only that, but our longing to commune with Him will be heightened as we are inspired to seek Him with our whole heart.

Chapter 4

SEARCH FOR HIM

*What comes into our minds when we think about
God is the most important thing about us.*
—A.W. TOZER, *The Knowledge of the Holy*

I want to know God is the cry of my heart. I want to know everything
about Him. I love thinking about what He looks like, how He acts, and
how He feels. There is nothing more exciting, in the quietness of my
soul, than to think about Him. His vastness is too great, His tenderness
is so sweet, and His majesty is so full of awe that I don't understand
Him. That's why I keep searching the deeper things of God.

As soon as I know something about God, I feel like I know nothing.
The revelation of what I received of Him today, far surpasses what I
knew of Him yesterday. For example, when I encounter His goodness, I
get a revelation of His greater goodness, and the last thing that I knew
of Him was so little compared to what I know now, that it propels me
to search Him out even more. I'm in a search for the knowledge of God.

C.H. Spurgeon puts it like this,

But while the subject humbles the mind, it also expands it.
He who often thinks of God, will have a larger mind than the

man who simply plods around this narrow globe…the most excellent study for expanding the soul, is the science of Christ, and Him crucified, and the knowledge of the Godhead in the glorious Trinity. Nothing will so enlarge the intellect, nothing so magnify the whole soul of man, as a devout, earnest, continued investigation of the great subject of the Deity.[1]

God is so glorious. I feel like I know nothing about Him, but that really doesn't matter. What matters is that I can't get enough of Him: I have to encounter the God of my soul! What matters most is the continual search for the knowledge of God.

We love Him because He first loved us (1 John 4:19).

What's captivating to me is that God first put the love in us that draws us to Him, and when we fall out of love or disconnected from Him, He draws us back to His heart. In our earthly, prideful mind we think it's us who is making the first step toward God, but quite the opposite. It's really our response to what we feel and to what He shows us. When He reveals an aspect of who He is, He is really drawing us to Himself. He may show the fear of the Lord to us, which is an aspect of who He is, and that draws us to Him. Likewise, when He shows us His kindness, it usually leads us to repentance, which really is encountering His heart for us, and therefore we respond with repentance.

What we need is a revelation of who He is. We need the knowledge of God to hit our hearts. We must seek to search God out in the study of God; but in the study of God, it must lead us to God.

J.I. Packer suggests that "As He is the subject of our study and our helper in it, so He must Himself be the end of it. It was for this purpose that revelation was given, and it is to this use that we must put it."[2] We must enlarge our understanding about God, not just the attributes about God, but with the living God, of whose attributes they really are. "A little knowledge of God is worth more than a great deal of knowledge about Him."[3]

Thus says the Lord: "Let not the wise man glory in his wisdom, let not the mighty man glory in his might, nor let the rich man glory in his riches; but let him who glories glory in this, that he understands and knows Me, that I am the Lord, exercising lovingkindness, judgment, and righteousness in the earth. For in these I delight," says the Lord (Jeremiah 9:23-24).

Journey with me into living a life committed to searching out the knowledge of God and the glory in knowing Him through experience. I believe God is calling every believer to the very depth of who He is. He is in essence beckoning us, "Come away with Me."

Let's be a people who seek the deepest parts of who He is. Let's survey the mountain of His majesty and walk through the rivers of God's infinite delight. With His help and His leadership, we will make every intention possible to draw near to God's heart. We were made for communion with Him by first knowing about Him and then responding to Him.

All throughout Scripture men and women have encountered an aspect of who God is, with each person responding differently, but consistently each response had the element of being "undone." Let me show you.

ISAIAH IS UNDONE

The prophet Isaiah had an awe-inspiring moment that more than likely changed his life. There are so many points to make in Isaiah 6, but I want to emphasize the impact on Isaiah when he saw the glory of God sitting on His throne in the heavenly temple. He saw the Lord sitting on the throne, high and lifted up, and the train of His robe filled the entire temple (see Isa. 6:1). He saw the seraphim, each one having six wings. Imagine that! Six wings—two of the wings to cover their face, two to cover their feet, and with the other two they flew (see Isa. 6:2). This is his response:

So I said, "Woe is me, for I am undone! Because I am a man of unclean lips, and I dwell in the midst of a people of unclean lips; for my eyes have seen the King, the Lord of hosts" (Isaiah 6:5).

In response to God's splendor, Isaiah saw his own uncleanliness. He's overwhelmed with his need to be transformed. This is a tremendous motivator to him. Sin appears foolish to him in that hour. It seems so minor compared to the majesty of God. Whenever we come in contact with God, or the knowledge of God touches us, foolish sin seems unreasonable and becomes like something we don't want anything to do with. We disassociate ourselves from sinful ways that once were part of our lives. We despise compromise when we encounter God and it gives us tremendous energy against sin.

This is quite an intense supernatural encounter. I'm not saying that you have to see God in an open vision. God can touch and overwhelm our hearts little by little and change our emotional chemistry just through meditating on the Word and spending time talking to Him. We don't necessarily have to have a full-on experience to have our hearts transformed.

I remember after one meeting in 2011 when I encountered both God's knowledge and His presence so intimately and in such a real way, that I was literally undone for any type of sin. In fact, I spent nights next to my bed asking God not to leave my physical body in such a tangible way.

That's one of the things that the knowledge of God does for us: it motivates us to depart from evil. That's what happened to Isaiah at the moment when He encountered God.

The words *"Woe is me, for I am undone"* are so powerful! In fact these words don't stop ringing in my heart even as I write this, because every person who encounters God at some level responds like this. The person is literally "undone" as I will show you through the life of Moses, Daniel, and Mary. They were undone by the very awe, holiness, majesty, and glorious attributes that satisfied them. It's more than just seeing the state of sin. It's much greater than that. When we encounter the God of heaven, sin and our sinful state are nothing in comparison. When we see how glorious and extraordinary God really is, it will leave our hearts and our bodies undone. It is worth repeating what A.W. Tozer wrote, "The man who comes to a right belief about God is relieved of ten thousand temporal problems."[4]

KNOWLEDGE OF HIM

Our minds can't fully comprehend who God really is. He really is unfathomable. There is no one like Him. God is infinite, and information about Him can come every second into our minds and we still would not be any closer than when we started. Reaching the full knowledge of God is impossible. I say again, our minds simply cannot comprehend or imagine how magnificent God is.

> When we try to imagine what God is like we must of necessity use that which is not God as the raw material for our minds to work on; hence whatever we visualize God to be, He is not, for we have constructed our image out of that which He has made and what He has made is not God. If we insist upon trying to imagine Him, we end with an idol, made not with hands but with thoughts; and an idol of the mind is as offensive to God as an idol of the hand.[5]

You will never be able to discover Him with your mind and intellect; it's only through your spirit that you can encounter Him—and this is done through faith. All the aspects of who you are help in that search, but it's only by your spirit that you can really begin to search and find the truths of who He is.

> *The heavens declare the glory of God; and the firmament shows His handiwork. Day unto day utters speech, and night unto night reveals knowledge. There is no speech nor language where their voice is not heard* (Psalm 19:1-3).

MOSES ASKS TO SEE GOD'S GLORY

Moses talked to God as a man speaks to a friend. He wanted God always with him, refusing to lead the Israelites without the presence of God. Moses wanted a deeper revelation of His presence, and he relentlessly and desperately asked God to *"show me Your glory"* (Exod. 33:18). This is God's response to Moses' request.

> *Then He said, "I will make all My goodness pass before you, and I will proclaim the name of the Lord before you. I will be gracious to whom I will be gracious, and I will have compassion on whom I will have compassion"* (Exodus 33:19).

Notice that God was going to have His goodness pass in front of Moses and have His name declared to him. Let's observe what Moses asked for. He wanted to see God's glory. In the Old Testament, one of the meanings of the word *glory* is translated as the weight of something, but it also speaks of splendor, abundance, and beauty. Moses didn't want to see God's power; he already had seen God's great power. In this encounter, the glory of God is the revelation of God's beauty. Notice what God reveals. He reveals His personality. He reveals His emotions. The pinnacle of God's glory in this passage is when God revealed His emotions to Moses.

Can you imagine what real goodness is? "The Hebrew word for goodness is *tuwb*. It means 'good in the widest sense.' In other words, nothing withheld."⁶ God's name and His personality are one and the same. God is the very essence of goodness, mercy, and compassion, and God was going to reveal this to Moses.

God has the best personality in the universe. God has the most kind, good, pure, happy, joyful, smart, mysterious, passionate, gentle, wise, and bold personality in all of existence.

The LORD passed before him and proclaimed, "The LORD, the LORD God, merciful and gracious, longsuffering, and abounding in goodness and truth" (Exodus 34:6).

When you think of someone's name, a flood of thoughts and emotions about that person comes to mind, good or bad. Their name and their personality are synonymous. When I think about my children, I know their names and I know their personalities. I know their weaknesses and their strengths. I know their victories and defeats. I know them, and their name represents who they are. The same is true of God. In this passage, God revealed His personality, His emotions; therefore you can call Him merciful. You can call Him gracious. He is longsuffering and abounding in goodness. He is not just good, He is the very center of where good comes from. God reveals His personality and His name at the same time.

God reveals four of His names to us in this passage in Exodus 34, which show us His personality. Every one of these aspects of God hold infinite truth to be searched out. Think about this for a second with me. One of His names is "The Lord is longsuffering." He bears long with us instead of "writing us off." He does not lose enthusiasm for us when we fail. He does not retaliate in the way people do. He suffers long with our sinful responses. His love for us is greater than the pain we cause Him when we resist Him. I urge you to meditate and know who God is.

Moses had a taste of God, but he simply wanted more. He was undone by the manifest presence and personality of God. At first look, you see that Moses didn't want to lead God's people without the very presence of God, but a taste of God's presence, reality, and beauty had Moses remain in His very presence for hours, days, and even weeks. He wanted to see and know more. Moses desired to see God's glory and beauty for himself over and over.

Have you ever thought of the goodness of God? His beauty is so attractive. His personality is so striking. This rocks Moses' world and understanding of God. If we would touch God's personality, we would also be truly undone.

Beholding God not only affected his heart, but also his physical appearance. When Moses came down the mountain after spending time with God, the skin of His face shone brighter than normal. This even brought fear on those who saw him, so he decided to put a veil over his face. The Bible says in Exodus 34:30, *"When Aaron and all the children of Israel saw Moses, behold, the skin of his face shone, and they were afraid to come near him."* This happened over and over again to Moses. Choose to behold God today. Everything about you will be different.

BEHOLDING GOD

But we all, with unveiled face, beholding as in a mirror the glory of the Lord, are being transformed into the same image from glory to glory, just as by the Spirit of the Lord (2 Corinthians 3:18).

This is one of my favorite portions of Scripture. This verse has so many abundant promises for us to take hold of. God has made a way to unveil our view, which means to be able to look at God with an open face. God has opened our hearts to see Him clearly and rightly, nothing veiling us. Jesus paid the price to tear down all veils and the Holy Spirit came to reside in us as the revealer of truth. This is a guarantee that if we behold Him, we will be transformed into the same image as Him, to look identical to Him. Imagine that?

The beholding as in a mirror, is speaking about looking at the glory of the Lord that is in us. The Holy Spirit resides in us and as we behold Him, we begin to reflect that glory that we behold.

This verse establishes the principle that we become what we behold. If we look on the sins of our outer selves, we will be enslaved to those sins; but if we behold the glory of the Lord within us, we will reflect that glory in our actions.

How do we do that practically? Beholding God's glory means to look at (study or encounter) His emotions, power, and wisdom as seen in creation, redemption, and His leadership over history. We practically behold Him by looking at His attributes and emotions and therefore shift our mind to see Him rightly. We begin this by meditating on who the Bible says He is and what He is like.

God shines in our hearts to reveal knowledge of His glory (see 2 Cor. 4:6). By reading Scripture we fill our minds with knowledge of God, then we turn the Word into a dialogue with God as we pray-read it. As we see Him rightly, our view of Him changes and therefore we change. If our image of God is viewed correctly, we begin to view ourselves correctly. I will discuss this later on.

DANIEL'S ANGEL ENCOUNTER

Daniel's name means "God is my judge." Daniel is one of the most incredible men in history who exemplified how to walk in the fear of God, instead of the fear of man. Daniel was a forerunner for living a life set apart in the midst of an anti-God culture. We are first introduced to Daniel as a young man of royal stock brought to Babylon in exile.

King Darius noticed the great wisdom and revelation of Daniel and made him ruler over the whole province of Babylon, and chief administrator over all the wise men of Babylon (see Dan. 2:48). He governed with a spirit of excellence, and at the same time had *"understanding in all visions and dreams"* (Dan. 1:17). Daniel had incredible encounters with God and the angelic realm, seeing amazing visions and having incredible visitations. Once while Daniel was with other men at a riverbank, an angel came down to visit him. This angel was majestic and powerful. He had the disposition that reflected God Himself, but was an angel. He was withstood for 21 days in warfare but he came to deliver the meaning of the message, in response to Daniel's prayer:

> *Therefore I was left alone when I saw this great vision, and no strength remained in me; for my vigor was turned to frailty in me, and I retained no strength. Yet I heard the sound of his words; and while I heard the sound of his words I was in a deep sleep on my face, with my face to the ground. Suddenly, a hand touched me, which made me tremble on my knees and on the palms of my hands* (Daniel 10:8-10).

This vision was so real and so powerful it caused those with Daniel to flee in terror and Daniel lost physical strength. *"My lord, because of the vision my sorrows have overwhelmed me, and I have retained no strength"* (Dan. 10:16).

Daniel lost all his strength, and his vigor was turned to frailty. Confronted by the glory of the messenger and the content of the vision, Daniel was reduced to nothing. The Hebrew word for glory, *"kabowd,"* means the great physical weight or quantity of a thing. When used in describing God's glory it means "imposing, weighty presence." All the nations will bow before His glory.[7]

> *The angel said to Daniel, "O Daniel, man greatly beloved, understand the words that I speak to you, and stand upright, for I have now been sent to you." While he was speaking this word to me, I stood trembling.* (Daniel 10:11).

Daniel, as a young man, lived for a higher resolve; he purposed in his heart not to eat the king's delicacies, showing that fasting from food was the battleground he chose to war against the culture of his day. He was strong in spirit and confident in the God he had seen and known. Daniel had a focused life and a life of faithful prayer. Daniel diligently beheld the Word of God; he knew the Scriptures and prayed over what he studied, therefore he lived differently. Daniel discovered how small the earth's largest empire is compared to the sovereign throne room of the living God. He was not intimidated by earthly kings. When you see God, you will risk everything, even death in a lion's den. You will speak when it could be dangerous, you will pray for everyone to see, even when it's outlawed to do so. You will refuse to worship anything other than God Almighty, for if you see and know God, you will live differently.

"Daniel gives us glimpses of the unseen contention for the purposes of God to be manifest in the historic moment and how prayer moves, shifts, and enables the breaking in of God's divine purposes."[8] When you see and know God, you will do anything when the divine vision hits your heart. You will count it a privilege to do anything for love! Daniel was a man who lived undone, not for a moment but for his entire life on earth!

JOHN'S REVELATION

John, the beloved, on the island of Patmos saw heaven in all its splendor, and got a revelation of Jesus, as He is today. This is one of the most profound, most descriptive views that we get of Jesus. The book of Revelation says that John saw Jesus. This is the clearest picture of what Jesus physically looks like and sounds like today. Take time to mediate on this.

Then I turned to see the voice that spoke with me. And having turned I saw seven golden lampstands, and in the midst of the seven lampstands One like the Son of Man, clothed with a garment down to the feet and girded about the chest with a golden band. His head and hair were white like wool, as white as snow, and His eyes like a flame of fire; His feet were like fine brass, as if refined in a furnace, and His voice as the sound of many waters; He had in His right hand seven stars, out of His mouth went a sharp two-edged sword, and His countenance was like the sun shining in its strength (Revelation 1:12-16).

When this man who walked with Jesus for three years saw the God-Man Jesus of today, he responds with such fear and trembling that he falls to the ground as though dead. The beloved disciple, who had handled the Word of life, sees the revelation of the majesty of God in the flesh and is literally undone. This is how he responded:

And when I saw Him, I fell at His feet as dead. But He laid His right hand on me, saying to me, "Do not be afraid; I am the First and the Last (Revelation 1:17).

Jesus can manifest or veil His resurrected glory according to the situation. He veiled it when He appeared in John 20-21. However, here in Revelation 1, He manifested His glory causing John to fall as a dead man. The manifestation of His glorious presence overwhelms John. This is the unrehearsed response of all who have been privileged to see the glory of the Lord. A person who is dead does not move. John was frozen stiff, lying on the ground as though he was dead. He simply couldn't move, he was undone.

The reason I am sharing these examples with you is to show you how necessary it is to pursue the knowledge of God. We know God through the experiential knowledge of God: He's infinite in His greatness. The knowledge of God brings forth the doctrine of incomprehensibility.

The doctrine of incomprehensibility simply means that God cannot be exhaustibly known in even one of His attributes.

Our present worship is too limited. If we could really see Him, we would worship Him more, we would purely be undone. God is infinitely great and Jesus is infinitely worthy. Let me show you an extravagant worshiper who lavishly expended costly perfume on the One she loved.

MARY'S EXTRAVAGANCE

Mary of Bethany is an extraordinary woman to me. I have asked myself questions from her story that I will ask you at the end.

> *Being in Bethany at the house of Simon...as He* [Jesus] *sat at the table, a woman* [Mary of Bethany; see John 12:3] *came having an alabaster flask of very costly oil of spike-nard* [perfume]. *She broke the flask and poured it on His head. Some* [apostles] *were indignant...and said, "Why was this...oil wasted? It might have been sold for...three hundred denarii* [a year's wages] *and given to the poor." They* [apostles] *criticized her sharply. Jesus said, "Let her alone...she has done a good work for Me. ...wherever this gospel is preached...what this woman has done will be told as a memorial to her"* (Mark 14:3-9).

This was a very costly act that Mary did. The perfume was worth 300 denarii (equivalent to a year's wages). Jesus told His disciples that He was to be crucified in two days (see Matt. 26:2). Mary seems to have been the only one who heard Him, and thus she poured her perfume on Him. The fragrance was on both of them at the cross.

> *Mary...wiped His feet with her hair. The house was filled with the fragrance...* (John 12:3).

Mary broke her most precious earthly treasure over the One who was her greatest treasure. The perfume was probably her inheritance, thus representing her financial security. I imagine her saying to her friends, "I have Jesus—He is everything to me. What else can I give Him?"

What is our response? Do we even have a response? Have we ever even known God, even a little, to respond in any way like John, Daniel, Mary, or Isaiah? Have we been undone?

UNDONE OVER AND OVER

For the most part we have departed from the glory of knowing God. We are not undone because we simply don't see, and we don't see because we are not searching Him out. We don't seek the God-Man Jesus between the lines of the Word of God. We don't ponder or meditate on the mysteries of God. We don't commune with the indwelling Spirit of God inside us. We don't search Him out. What are we to do? The answer is simple, it's not complicated if we would simply do it. To this issue A.W. Tozer says, "It is simply the old and ever new counsel: Acquaint thyself with God. To regain her lost power the Church must see heaven opened and have a transforming vision of God."[9]

> If you seek her as silver, and search for her as for hidden treasures (Proverbs 2:4).

We must be willing to pay any price in our quest to search for God, as for hidden treasure. If we can live without more of God, then we will go without more of God. We must spend long hours in our quest to search after God. We search for Him like a covetous person searches after wealth.

SEARCH FOR HIM—THE EASY PART

Searching and knowing God is the easiest and the most difficult objective in life to reach. It's easy because it's not done with our intellect, where you can try to figure out the complexities and mysteries of God as in a science experiment and come up with some easy conclusion. Humankind has been doing that for centuries and falling into the same plain foolishness. The pursuit of the knowledge of God cannot be done without Him unveiling Himself to us. God almighty has to reveal God Almighty, or whatever aspect He wants to show us.

Searching out the knowledge of God is easy because it is "something freely given. As sunlight falls free on the open field, so the knowledge of the holy God is a free gift to men who are open to receive it."[10] God illuminates Himself to our hearts if we are in pursuit of Him. If we are in pursuit of knowledge as an end to itself, we will end up short because *"Knowledge puffs up..."* (1 Cor. 8:1).

SEARCH FOR HIM—THE DIFFICULT PART

The difficult part in seeking Him is that there are some conditions, or a better way to put it is that there is a certain posture of the heart that we must have. I would like to define some of those postures to help us in our pursuit of God, while in the pursuit of knowledge.

Postures of the Heart—Purity

> *Blessed are the pure in heart, for they shall see God* (Matthew 5:8).

The first posture that our hearts must be set in is purity. Purity includes pursuit of holiness, not simply in outward motions but in the heart motivations and methods. There is no substitute for purity for those who want to see God. Great blessings come as we pursue a life of purity. The best part of positioning ourselves in purity is that God empowers us through His grace when we simply posture our hearts there. Even this is not done by our own will; but in our resolve to pursue, God comes in with His power to help us in our weakness.

The ultimate experience of Christianity, now and for eternity, is to know and see God (see Rev. 22:4). The reality of seeing God is the highest privilege that a human being can experience. The pure in heart will have an increased capacity to see and experience God. The promise is there: we will see God if we walk in purity. Purity does not "earn" revelation of God, but positions us so our spiritual capacity is enlarged to experience and see God.

Are there areas of deliberate disobedience in your life? Deliberate sin blocks spiritual progress and hinders your walk with the Lord. Make a consistent resolution to confess and resist sinful areas. Realize that God looks more at the sincerity of your motives to obey than at your actual attainment of spiritual maturity.

Postures of the Heart—Obedience

> *He who has My commandments and keeps them, it is he who loves Me* (John 14:21).

Another important posture of the heart is to set ourselves to live a life of obedience. "Jesus called us to be perfect in our obedience that is to be mature or complete in it. This is meant to be the primary issue in our spiritual life yet it is often overlooked and disregarded. We do this by seeking to walk in all the light that the Spirit gives us. The pursuit of full obedience is not the same as attaining it. Our pursuit for complete obedience is relative in this age and absolute in the age-to-come. Our responsibility is to focus on 'seeking' to completely obey God. We trust God's grace to empower us to 'attain' full obedience in an ever-increasing measure."[11]

> *You shall be perfect* [walk in all the light you receive] *just as your Father in heaven is perfect* (Matthew 5:48).

Even in this, God is looking for the posture of your heart to be on Him. He's not looking for outward perfection, but inward grasping. If your inner struggle is toward Him, He is able to come in and help you. He recognizes that your heart is set on knowing Him, and He comes in agreement with your "yes" no matter how weak it may seem. It's a resounding "yes" to His heart.

> *We also have as our ambition…to be pleasing to Him* (2 Corinthians 5:9 NASB).

Paul said it clearly in the NKJV, *"We make it our aim…to be well-pleasing to Him."* There was a moment in Paul's life where he consciously determined this would be the primary dream of his life. He determined this would be the supreme preoccupation of his life, walking with the Lord and living his entire life to be well pleasing to Him. To *"make it his aim"* means it is the primary reason for why he had life on the earth.[12]

The apostle Paul was preoccupied with Jesus' evaluation of him. It is what drove Paul and motivated him to run the race with endurance.[13]

Postures of the Heart—Intentional Dialogue

Intimacy with God is the knowledge of God. Experiential and emotional knowledge is what cultivates intimacy. The more you know of a person's heart and mind, you fall in love in a more intimate way. Therefore, knowledge begets intimacy. In his book *Practicing the Presence of God*, Brother Lawrence says, "We have to know someone before we can truly love him. In order to know God, we must think about Him often. Once we get to know Him, we will think about Him even more often, because where our treasure is, there also is our heart!"[14]

> *But as it is written: "Eye has not seen, nor ear heard, nor have entered into the heart of man the things which God has prepared for those who love Him." But God has revealed*

them to us through His Spirit. For the Spirit searches all things, yes, the deep things of God. For what man knows the things of a man except the spirit of the man which is in him? Even so no one knows the things of God except the Spirit of God (1 Corinthians 2:9-11).

One of the central postures of the heart, or keys to intimacy, is to cultivate a relationship with the Holy Spirit. It's simply impossible without Him. The Holy Spirit is the divine escort to revelation. He longs to show us and declare knowledge to us, leading to the deeper things of God. It's Holy Spirit who escorts you to knowledge, to Jesus.

Postures of the Heart—Meditating

The next posture that we must give ourselves to is the practice of meditating on the Word of God. This is an attribute of communion with God that will take time and effort. It takes diligence, consistency, and focus. It is important for me to emphasize that the renewal of our mind is a process that requires significant time and effort on our part.

I speak about meditating on the Word several times throughout this book because I find it of the utmost significance and must stress it again. We must feed ourselves on the truths of the written Word and then incorporate them into our prayer lives consistently over time. "As we set our lives before the Word of God, we will always find delight and joy in the eternal Word who lives inside of us."[15]

> *If you will...treasure my commands* [Word] *within you* (Proverbs 2:1 NASB).

God commands us to treasure His Word. We treasure God's commandments (His Word) as we fill our minds with His Word. We dialogue with Jesus as a Person by conversing with Him through prayer as we meditate on the Scriptures. It is impossible to grow in intimacy with Jesus without regular meditation on the Scripture.

We purposefully use our time to fill our mind with the Word of God so that our emotions are affected. Without this part of God's grace, we will never grow substantially.

> *The natural man does not receive the things of the Spirit of God, for they are foolishness to him; nor can he know them, because they are spiritually discerned* (1 Corinthians 2:14).

The man who would know God must give time to Him. He must count no time wasted, which is spent in the cultivation of His acquaintance. He must give himself to meditation and prayer hours on end.[16]

WARFARE IN KNOWLEDGE

The central issue of spiritual warfare is around the knowledge of God. The fight of the ages is the fight over truth. How much truth we know and walk in determines our success. The Church is a powerful force when we grow in the knowledge of God. Satan assaults the knowledge of God by blinding people's eyes to it (see 2 Cor. 4:4). Hosea 4:6 says that God's people are destroyed or perish for a lack of knowledge. The lack of the knowledge of God is what constitutes strongholds. Lies built up and believed upon create a stronghold that allows the devil to govern and have access into our lives.

> *Whose minds the god of this age* [satan] *has blinded…lest the light…of the glory of Christ…should shine on them. For we do not preach ourselves, but Christ Jesus…. For it is the God who commanded light to shine out of darkness, who has shone in our hearts to give the light of the knowledge of the glory of God in the face* [Person] *of Jesus Christ* (2 Corinthians 4:4-6).

Satan's number one job description is to accuse the heart of God and the heart of the believer. Night and day satan is accusing God to your heart (see Rev. 12:10). His goal is to distort the truth of the knowledge of God within your own heart so that you're confused about what God thinks and feels when He looks at you and thinks about you. If you get wrong ideas about the personality of God and the image of God, you'll get wrong ideas about your own image and your own spiritual identity before God. Let me explain this significant truth.

THOUGHTS OF GOD DETERMINE WHO WE ARE

One of my most favorite quotes comes from A.W. Tozer in his book *The Knowledge of the Holy:* "What comes into our minds when we think about God is the most important thing about us."[17]

I feel this quote is so important because of what I experienced first-hand as a father. I recently took a 2-week trip to the Philippines with our Pursuit Internship program participants. I took my 8-year-old son Elijah with me. We saw healings, miracles, and more than 4,000 salvations. But what marked my heart the most about the trip was seeing my son spend so much time examining me. He put his fingers next to mine. He bent my fingers and bent his right next to mine. He looked at my elbows, my facial features, and was constantly comparing himself to me. What my son knows about his father is so important to understanding his own identity as my son.

Also, he is proud to be an American, not because he has American memories, he was born there and only lived there until he was six months old. But because I am proud to be an American, so is he. When the presidential elections happen, all my children ask, "What are we, Dad? Are we Democrats or Republicans?" They only care about the elections because I do and they will fight and contend for any side that I do. It's the same with us. What we know about God and what we think about God is the most important thing about us. Therefore pursuing the knowledge of God is of the utmost importance to knowing Him in the most intimate way possible.

I would encourage you to take some time and consider what you think about God. Don't say all the religious words to describe God. Take some time, in quietness, and consider your thoughts about God. How do you view Him? What is He like to you? How does He respond when you make a mistake? How does He respond when you do something good? Is He usually mostly glad or mostly frustrated with you? This exercise will determine a lot about you. How you see and think about God is the most important thing about you.

In discovering more about God, we discover more about us. So pursuing the knowledge of God is not only about knowing God, inasmuch as it is about discovering who we are in God.

KNOWLEDGE OF GOD FILLS THE EARTH

For the earth will be filled with the knowledge of the glory of the Lord, as the waters cover the sea (Habakkuk 2:14).

In closing this chapter, I believe that God is calling this generation—you, me, and those who are children now—to be seekers of the knowledge of God. The earth will be filled with the knowledge of the glory of God. The knowledge of what God is like will fill the earth (Hab. 2:14).

It's fantastic! The entire population of the earth will encounter the knowledge of God. This is our journey now and forever!

Chapter 5

DECLARE THE FATHER

I will be a Father to you, and you will be my sons…
—Father God

On December 21, 2012, my wife Christelle gave birth to our sixth child. She was 16 weeks pregnant when we discovered our son didn't have a heartbeat. We battled with so many emotions and questions. The next day she gave birth to a very small baby boy whom we named Benjamin Micah. He had already gone to be with his Father in heaven. Learning of his death, then going through the birth and burial of his body, our hearts were extremely sad. Our other five children also went through their own sadness and they each wrote letters, which we buried with Benjamin. Our family united like never before as we cried, prayed, and released our son and their brother to our heavenly Father and the leadership of Jesus.

Days afterward were filled with so many thoughts of what could have been: the first giggle, the first steps, his smile, and much more. A month later, I went to the gym with our three older children. When I took their gym cards out of my pocket it felt like I was missing one, but I had all of the gym cards in my hand. I knew what was missing, the possibility of seeing and holding my other son's gym card. We mourned and ached for what could have been, more than anything. Oh, the deep pain of missing and desiring to be with our son were beyond words! I barely held him and barely saw his features. I had only one day with him, and even though he was not alive, I knew he was my son.

FAMILY—THE GREATEST PRIVILEGE

We have a busy lifestyle leading a growing ministry, raising five kids, and maintaining a spiritual walk. Christelle and I have a marriage that is made in heaven and we love our friendship. The greatest thing that we get to enjoy together is raising and nurturing our family. They are all so beautiful and precious to me. My eyes even well up writing this. As you can tell, one of my favorite things to do in this life is to lead and serve my family. I absolutely love being a father.

...the glory of children is their father (Proverbs 17:6).

With each of the births of my children I have been asked, "How can you love this next child as much as the others?" The question is absurd to my heart. Each child, with their distinct personality, creates something so special and unique that I could not imagine life without any one of them. I can only imagine what God the Father feels over His sons and daughters, over His children.

God has millions of children who are all His favorites. Every one of them is the apple of His eye. You are His beloved son or daughter whom He loves with a passion.

UNDERSTANDING THE HEART OF THE FATHER

Behold, I will send you Elijah the prophet before the coming of the great and dreadful day of the Lord. And he will turn the hearts of the fathers to the children, and the hearts of the children to their fathers... (Malachi 4:5-6).

I want to talk to you in this chapter about one of the most important paradigm shifts that I believe we need to have in order to understand the heart of the Father rightly. If we don't view God the Father rightly, we won't come near to Him; therefore, we won't commune with Him. Many want to know God personally but they view Him as a remote and impersonal Being. Usually we, as humans, shy away from what we don't know. I would also add that if we don't understand the Father rightly, it directly affects our identity. If we don't know who we are as a son or daughter, we live aimless lives, not knowing who we are and where we are going. Many Christians are really living as orphans or Fatherless when they have the most amazing Father ready for full embrace.

To add to the point of our identity as sons and daughters, I believe that one of the most significant prophetic moves the Holy Spirit is doing is found in Malachi 4:6. The Holy Spirit is turning the hearts of the children to our heavenly Father. I believe the Holy Spirit is doing this to our earthly Fathers, but more importantly He is drawing us to our heavenly Father.

Let me begin by defining what a father is by looking at the meaning of the word. Father: *the founder of a race, family, or line, originator. Someone who exercises paternal care over other persons, paternal protector or provider, a person who has originated or established something.*[1]

Our heavenly Father is all of that and much more. Throughout this chapter we will observe how many view the Father and how Jesus wants us to view Him.

Many view God the Father as a grumpy, disgruntled, and frustrated God. These misconceptions affect a big part of our lives and can cause us to live in performance mode, trying to please a God who is mostly angry or mostly unhappy with us.

> *The Spirit you received does not make you slaves, so that you live in fear again; rather, the Spirit you received brought*

about your adoption to sonship. And by him we cry, "Abba, Father" (Romans 8:15 NIV).

THE FATHER REVEALED IN HUMAN FORM

As soon as humankind fell from the covering of God, the entire Godhead began planning a rescue plan. God the Father wanted His family, and He created a plan to bring His family together under His covering once again.

John 14:5-6 records one of the most important statements in the entire New Testament. Here we read that Thomas asked Jesus a question.

> *Thomas said to Him, "Lord, we do not know where You are going, and how can we know the way?" Jesus said to him, "I am the way, the truth, and the life. No one comes to the Father except through Me"* (John 14:5-6).

Because we have heard these verses many times before, we can tend to overlook their significance and meaning. Jesus is, in essence, expressing His oneness with the Father. Jesus is also showing us that He is the signpost to the Father. The first thing Jesus said is that He is *The Way*: Jesus' death on the cross made a way for us to go to the Father by paying the debt of our sin on the cross to give us access to relationship with the Father in this age (see Eph. 2:18). Through this, He is revealing that the Father's heart is being shown through His human Son.

John Eldredge, in his book *Fathered by God,* says, "You are the son of a kind, strong, and engaged Father, a Father wise enough to guide you in the Way, generous enough to provide for your journey. His first act of provision happened before you were even born, when He rescued you through the life, death, resurrection...Jesus of Nazareth...At the core of them is a coming into true sonship."[2]

In summary: We obtain forgiveness through the death of Jesus Christ, by His atonement for our sins. Let's not miss the ultimate goal however.

Forgiveness is not the end result. A relationship with the Father is the ultimate goal. If we don't understand what it means to be a son or daughter of God the Father, we haven't understood Christianity. The goal is to have our identity firmly established in being a son and daughter of the Father.

> *Because you are his sons, God sent the Spirit of his Son into our hearts, the Spirit who calls out, "Abba, Father." So you are no longer a slave, but God's child; and since you are his child, God has made you also an heir* (Galatians 4:6-7 NIV).

Jesus showed the way to the Father through His death. He is the truth about how the Father relates (see John 14:7-24); and He is the life source to sustain this relationship (see John 15:1-11). Jesus came to make a way for us to relate to the Father forever and to show what the Father is like and how He desires to relate. Jesus continues...

> *If you had known Me, you would have known My Father also; and from now on you know Him and have seen Him* (John 14:7).

I think the words that are crucial and carry much weight are the words, *"from now on."* I believe Jesus is saying, I'm revealing Him to you at this very moment and the way you view Him will never be the same again.

Then Philip says to Jesus, *"Show us the Father"* (John 14:8). The Father speaks through Jesus at that very moment. I encourage you to take special notice how Jesus responds in the past tense. Jesus says:

> *Anyone who has seen me has seen the Father. How can you say, "Show us the Father"?* (John 14:9 NIV)

> *Then Jesus answered and said to them, "Most assuredly, I say to you, the Son can do nothing of Himself, but what He sees*

the Father do; for whatever He does, the Son also does in like manner (John 5:19).

Everything up until that point has shown the heart of the Father through what Jesus said and did. To that end, Jesus did miracles and showed compassion, reflecting only what He saw the Father do. He spoke powerfully and tenderly, but He only spoke what He heard the Father already say. So, in essence, He revealed the heart of the Father through everything that He did and said.

Jack Hayford states:

> Jesus wanted His disciples to grasp the fact that, for the whole time they had been together, He had lived in an unbroken, perfect link with Father God because of His own unique relationship as Son. Jesus had never spoken from His own authority but only as a direct expression of the Father's will, and He consistently affirmed that His works were not His, but the Father's (John 9:4; 10:37-38; 14:10).[3]

Jesus' words are even more pointed in John 10:30, where He says explicitly, *"I and My Father are one."* This provides a gateway into our exploration of how Jesus embodies the different names of God. All the attributes of the Father are reflected and demonstrated in the person and ministry of Christ.[4]

JESUS' DESIRE

I want us to look at another significant verse showing Jesus' desire to reveal the Father. It's found in John 17:24-26:

> *Father, I desire that they also whom You gave Me may be with Me where I am, that they may behold My glory which You have given Me; for You loved Me before the foundation of the world. O righteous Father! The world has not known*

You, but I have known You; and these have known that You sent Me. And I have declared to them Your name, and will declare it, that the love with which You loved Me may be in them, and I in them.

Here we find Jesus praying to the Father in heaven. Can you see the great emotion of this prayer that Jesus is crying out with? He has much desire here, but let's focus on His desire to reveal the Father. This is His prayer before He goes to the cross, and He deeply desires for humankind to know the Father. He cries out, O righteous Father! The world doesn't know you. So many people have a wrong view of God the Father; many have a distorted view of who He is, mostly because of the imperfect father figures we have on earth. Obviously, not all fathers have been abusive and hurtful. I had a wonderful father who loved me and gave generously. But just like my own earthly father, I have been a weak father in areas. So this can cause us to view our heavenly father in the same light. In his book *The Father Heart of God,* Floyd McClung notes, "Our past experiences color our responses when God reaches out to us."[5]

It was Jesus' desire for us to know the Father and to view Him rightly. Jesus wanted to change the view of the Father. Up until this point, Israel rightly viewed God as the transcendent Creator, but they were focused on His great power and holiness, worshiping Him at a distance. Jesus' desires and teachings showed that their great God was also their Father, to whom they were to draw near with confidence and assurance that He enjoyed them.

Our greatest emotional need is to have the assurance that God enjoys us even in our weakness. Every person was created with a longing to be delighted in and enjoyed by God. A prevailing stronghold in many people's lives today is related to the fear of rejection and the trauma of shame. This stronghold hinders our ability to enjoy God, His Word, and the work of the kingdom.

So I encourage you even right now to ask the Holy Spirit to reveal the Father to you and agree with this powerful prayer of Jesus.

A NEW PERSPECTIVE

I want to show you how Jesus presented the Father to us. Jesus reveals God's personality and how He pursues us, enjoys us, shows us great mercy, and feels deep affection as He rejoices over us. The truth that Jesus most emphasizes is that God rejoices as He restores people to Himself.

> *Then He said: "A certain man had two sons. And the younger of them said to his father, 'Father, give me the portion of goods that falls to me.' So he divided to them his livelihood. And not many days after, the younger son gathered all together, journeyed to a far country, and there wasted his possessions with prodigal living. But when he had spent all, there arose a severe famine in that land, and he began to be in want. Then he went and joined himself to a citizen of that country, and he sent him into his fields to feed swine. And he would gladly have filled his stomach with the pods that the swine ate, and no one gave him anything.*
>
> *"But when he came to himself, he said, 'How many of my father's hired servants have bread enough and to spare, and I perish with hunger! I will arise and go to my father, and will say to him, "Father, I have sinned against heaven and before you, and I am no longer worthy to be called your son. Make me like one of your hired servants."'*
>
> *"And he arose and came to his father. But when he was still a great way off, his father saw him and had compassion, and ran and fell on his neck and kissed him. And the son said to him, 'Father, I have sinned against heaven and in your sight, and am no longer worthy to be called your son.'*

"But the father said to his servants, 'Bring out the best robe and put it on him, and put a ring on his hand and sandals on his feet. And bring the fatted calf here and kill it, and let us eat and be merry; for this my son was dead and is alive again; he was lost and is found.' And they began to be merry" (Luke 15:11-24).

This story begins by showing us that the younger son takes his inheritance. He runs off and squanders it. If you were a father and had an inheritance to give, potentially a life savings that was worth a great deal, and you gave it to your son or daughter and they throw it away, how would you respond?

Jesus shows us how the Father in heaven responded to His son. I believe Jesus showed us this to reveal the Father's heart and for us to understand how to view Him rightly. I pray that through this you will see the heart of the Father in heaven, and how He responds to us in our weakness and speaks to our identity.

OUR FATHER'S RESPONSE

Jesus described how His Father responds and feels when His people repent.

And he arose and came to his father. But when he was still a great way off, his father saw him and had compassion, and ran and fell on his neck and kissed him (Luke 15:20).

- *He saw:* First of all, take a look at the father's expectancy and anticipation of the son's return. The father watched earnestly for the return of his son. This is a very comforting picture. The father was looking for the son's return. Having no idea when, this heartbroken father must have been looking down the road every day, hoping and praying for his son to return. Can you picture it? His eyes were set at a distance, longing to have his son back. This gives a picture of the father not only *not* forgetting, but yearning, missing and waiting. His heart is seized with the agony of the absence of his son.

- *He had compassion:* Another aspect of that father's heart for his son is, as you can see, that he had great compassion for him. The heavenly Father feels compassion over the prodigals on the day they repent. The newly repentant yet immature prodigal son had many areas that needed transformation. This is an overflowing expression of how our heavenly Father feels. He completely understands what we have done. Our sin and foolishness don't surprise Him. In fact, the wasted inheritance wasn't even brought up with the earthly father, nor our heavenly Father. The Father is full of compassion, filled with great emotion, and focused only on having his sons and daughters back. God doesn't turn a blind eye at rebellion. But to those with a repentant heart and who want to be with Him, He understands where they have been and is overcome with compassion. He welcomes them back in, He watches, waits and runs toward them.

- *He ran:* The father ran to his son. The son probably was shocked to see this, since a father in the ancient world did not usually run like this. We see God's enthusiasm for us; I love envisioning our Father running to us.

- *He fell on his neck:* The father embraced him affectionately instead of being repulsed and angry. He's affectionate. This is not a duty, but a privilege. I can only imagine how the father felt thinking his son was gone forever and then to have him come back. It had to be exhilarating!

His only response was to run to him and hug his neck, and that is exactly what God did. This was not a controlled, half-hearted, duty-based hug, but an aggressive, affection-based hug full of longing.

- *He kissed him:* The father's kiss signified the restoration of favor without a season of probation.

God does not confuse spiritual immaturity with rebellion. God loves unbelievers, but He both *loves* and *enjoys* believers. He immediately rejoices over us at the time of our repentance. He smiles over us as we begin the growth process with repentance, long before we attain maturity.

This parable is not primarily about a son who squandered his inheritance, but about a father who lost his son and how the father receives his son back.

God feels gladness over His returning prodigals and restores them to His favor (see Luke 15:24). We see this in the way the father, in this parable, gave his son the best robe and family ring on the day he returned.

But the father said to his servants, "Bring out the best robe and put it on him, and put a ring on his hand and sandals on his feet. And bring the fatted calf here and kill it, and let us eat and be merry; for my son was dead and is alive again...." They began to be merry (Luke 15:22-24).

- *Best robe:* These were reserved for honored guests (see Isa. 61:10).

- *Ring:* Authority was entrusted to him to represent the family business in the community.

- *Sandals:* Slaves did not have sandals; only the children received family privileges.

- *Fatted calf:* A calf was killed for special occasions and provided meat for over 50 guests.

- *Be merry:* The father called all to celebrate the recovery and return of his son.

SPEAKS DIRECTLY TO OUR IDENTITY

We can also see in this parable, that the son doesn't feel worthy to even be called a son. He felt lost in his identity. He would be content to be a servant. The father, however, doesn't even respond to what his son says. The father ignores his statement that he is *"no longer worthy to be called your son."* The father speaks directly into his identity by giving him his robe and invites him immediately back to him. The robe in the story is one reserved for the honored guest. Wow! From riches to rags, back to riches. He is given the family ring—a symbol of authority, and sandals. He is instantly lifted out of his miserable state and reinstated to his rightful place as his son.

There was no probation period, no waiting time to see if he was good enough, no trying to earn his way back in. He was immediately reinstated and restored to be his son. Imagine that! It's amazing that he was fully restored into his family and received into his father's arms and given the rightful place as if he was never gone.

This should be our primary view of the Father and this is the right view of the Father. He is slow to anger and full of compassion. He loves generously, forgives easily, and keeps no record of wrongs. He deeply desires His sons and daughters to have their identity firmly established as His children and He as their good Father. This is our Father, this is our God. Jesus Himself showed us the correct view we are to have of our Father through this amazing scene presented in this story.

I believe this was Jesus' primary message and central theme of His life on earth. I also believe this is one of the prayers He prays even today—that we would understand the Father rightly.

If a son asks for bread from any father among you, will he give him a stone? Or if he asks for a fish, will he give him a serpent instead of a fish? Or if he asks for an egg, will he offer him a scorpion? If you then, being evil, know how to give good gifts to your children, how much more will your heavenly Father give the Holy Spirit to those who ask Him!
(Luke 11:11-13)

Through this verse we see Jesus revealing the heart of the Father and asking us to compare the heavenly Father to our earthly fathers. He showed that any decent earthly father gives and provides for their children, but cannot compare to Father God. He is speaking to some of our greatest doubts and fears. I want to remind you that you are more valuable than all the birds of the air and all the fish of the sea. God provides for them daily. He provides and gives you the greatest gifts; and one of those gifts that makes a way and provides for us is the gift of the Holy Spirit.

As I end this chapter, I want to encourage you to ask the Holy Spirit to reveal the Father to you and to your heart. You are not fatherless. You are not an orphan. You are the apple of His eye and He longs to be with you. I pray that you gain the confidence to go straight to your Father who loves you and has made every way possible so you could run to Him today.

Chapter 6

THE MYSTERY OF JESUS

I have one passion. It is He, only He.
—COUNT ZINZENDORF

The mysteries of God are infinite. Our minds can hardly fathom the frontiers of who God is. The mystery of God Himself is difficult to communicate with human language. I certainly don't have the words to describe God. I am humbled at even my best effort. Our sincerest efforts to try to grasp the incomprehensible mysteries of God are forever unreachable with our human minds. Job said:

> *Can you fathom the mysteries of God? Can you probe the limits of the Almighty? They are higher than the heavens above—what can you do? They are deeper than the depths below—what can you know? Their measure is longer than the earth and wider than the sea* (Job 11:7-9 NIV).

The doctrine of the Trinity is a mystery of infinite and eternal proportions. If our minds can hardly explain the natural phenomenon of the hatching of an egg or the rising of the sun every morning and its going down every evening, we can hardly explain the mystery of the Trinity.

The mystery of the Godhead, three in one, is too marvelous to comprehend. With our human minds we are driven to try to make sense of three Persons in One.

In his book *The Knowledge of the Holy*, A.W. Tozer says, "The Persons of the Godhead, being one, have one will. They work always together, and never one smallest act is done by one without the instant acquiescence of the other two. Every act of God is accomplished by the Trinity in Unity."[1]

The mysteries of God are to be searched out as a person seeking treasures. The Kingdom of heaven has many mysteries that should be searched and found. For the child of God, they are not hidden from us but for us. They have *"been given to you to know the mysteries of the kingdom of heaven..."* (Matt. 13:11).

THE ALPHA AND OMEGA

A mystery of God that fascinates me is Jesus Himself. The last book of the Bible, the book of Revelation, is not meant to be a mystery but is meant to reveal Jesus to us.

A great Bible teacher and a good friend, Corey Stark explains:

> The book of Revelation is about the glory of a Man, the wisdom of His plan, and the power of His hand! In Revelation 1 Jesus is revealed, as the "Son of Man," highlighting 52 distinct aspects of His majesty, strategically given in 14 titles, 10 attributes and 28 descriptions, giving us the clearest picture of who Jesus is. Even as it takes time for our eyes to adjust so that we can see in a dark room, we will begin to see more detail about Jesus the longer we gaze upon these truths.
>
> These 52 distinct aspects of Jesus' majesty are merely hints that "whisper" of the infinite Person of the eternal God, increasing according to our hunger for more (Matt. 5:6). Each facet of

Jesus' majesty is only the tip of a massive iceberg of truth that the Holy Spirit will use to guide us into the deeper things of God if we have the courage to follow (1 Cor. 2:9-12)."[2]

In the book of Revelation, Jesus first defined Himself by *"saying, 'I am the Alpha and the Omega, the First and the Last'"* (Rev. 1:11).

He calls Himself "Alpha and Omega"—the first and last letters of the Greek alphabet. In the alphabet, one cannot speak of anything (or nothing) before alpha. There is no "before" alpha in the alphabet. Nor can one speak of anything (or nothing) after omega. There is no "after" omega in the alphabet.

So it is with God and reality. There is no "before" God and no "after" God. He is absolutely there, no matter how far back or how far forward you go. He is the absolute Reality. He has the honor of being there first and always.[3]

The Lion and the Lamb

Another one of my ultimate favorite portions of Scripture is Revelation 4 and 5. I could get lost in that scene for hours because I get a front-row view of the heavenly temple. It's truly majestic, and I get astonished with the reality that this scene is taking place right now at this very moment.

In Revelation 5, we see that there was a scroll that was sealed with seven seals and no one was found to be worthy to open it—no one in heaven, on earth, nor under the earth. Here God reveals another facet of His glorious mystery as the Lion and the Lamb.

No one was found worthy to be able to look inside the scroll and the apostle John begins to weep because no one was found worthy. But an elder said to him *"Do not weep. Behold, the Lion of the tribe of Judah, the Root of David, has prevailed to open the scroll and to loose its seven seals"* (Rev. 5:5).

So right here, we see Jesus as a lion. Then John looked and he saw in the *"midst of the throne and of the four living creatures, and in the midst of the elders, stood a Lamb as though it had been slain..."* (Rev. 5:6). This is a great mystery. How could the same lion be a lamb? "A lion is admirable for its ferocious strength and imperial appearance. A lamb is admirable for its meekness and servant-like provision of wool for our clothing. But even more admirable is a lion-like lamb and a lamb-like lion."[4]

Considering this for a minute makes us want to search Him out.

> We marvel at Him because his uncompromising justice is tempered with mercy. His majesty is sweetened by meekness... though he is worthy of all good; he was patient to suffer evil. His sovereign dominion over the world was clothed with a spirit of obedience and submission. He baffled the proud scribes with his wisdom, but was simple enough to be loved by children. He could still the storm with a word, but would not strike the Samaritans with lightning or take himself down from the cross.[5]

Jesus is both a lion and a lamb. He's the Lamb of God who takes away the sins of the whole earth (see John 1:29). He is also the lion who has defeated death, with great boldness and power, redeeming humankind for all of history.

> So the Lion is a lamb—an animal that is weak and harmless and lowly and easily preyed upon, and sheared naked for clothes, and killed for our food. So Christ is a lamb-like Lion. The Lion of Judah conquered because he was willing to act the part of a lamb.[6]

> This quality of meekness alone would not be glorious. The gentleness and humility of the lamb-like Lion become brilliant alongside the limitless and everlasting authority of the lion-like Lamb.[7]

Our Jesus had full authority over all powers, yet laid His life down like a lamb for us. This is a picture of who Jesus is, revealing Himself as the Lion and the Lamb.

WHO IS JESUS?

The mystery that you and I will search out for all eternity is Jesus, who is fully God and fully man. He fascinates me and I want to know Him. Our hearts are made to encounter Him through knowing Him.

> *...the people who know their God shall be strong* [vibrant in inner self], *and carry out great exploits. And those of the people who understand shall instruct many...* (Daniel 11:32-33).

The most important question in your life that you can ask yourself is *who do you say that Jesus is?* This is a vital question because you have to know who it is that you are encountering. What comes into your mind when you think about Jesus? Take a moment and ask yourself this question. When it's just you and Him. What do you see, what do you think about when you think about Jesus?

Well, you might say, "He created everything, He forgave me of my sin. He gave me eternal life, and sometimes He helps me out with money or something like that." To be honest, most people don't think too much about Jesus. Our thoughts are too few and our thoughts are way too low. People have a level of appreciation for Jesus of course, and sincere Christians worship Him in church, but they hardly think of Him outside of the allocated times.

How we view God matters. Many see Jesus as if He were a great yet distant king, whose primary interest in us is to save us so that we will praise Him and work for Him. The Gospel flourishes most when we understand the passion in God's personality for partnership with us. It is not enough to know what He has done for us. We need to know why He does what He does.

A.W. Tozer really provoked some of these thoughts in me: "The gravest question before the Church is always God Himself, and the most impactful fact about any man is not what he does with his time or what he says and does, but what he deep in his heart thinks about what God is like."[8]

One of the most important problems that we have is the lack of knowing and seeing who Jesus really is. A right concept of God is basic not only to know what we believe to create our theology, but understanding who He is will lead us to encounter Him and fellowship with Him. So what we need is to see Him more clearly. We need to see Him rightly. When our hearts are touched by who this God is, we experience much more than just the assurance that our sins have been forgiven or a warm feeling of blessedness. Knowing who He is will impact our hearts.

> To me…grace was given that I should preach…the unsearchable riches of Christ (Ephesians 3:8).

Paul says in Ephesians 3 that he will preach the unsearchable riches of Christ. Imagine this for a minute with me: *if we can see what the apostle Paul saw, we would live like Paul lived.* So what we need in this hour is a heart revelation of Jesus. It's an issue of seeing because there's a dynamic correlation between seeing and responding to Him.

FULLY GOD, FULLY MAN

Now I want to dive into how Jesus revealed Himself. There is nothing better than God revealing God to us. The title Jesus used in the Gospels most often about Himself is that He is the Son of Man (85 references). This title is referencing Daniel's prophecy of the Messiah who would rule all the nations:

I was watching in the night visions, and behold, One like the Son of Man, coming with the clouds of heaven! He came to the Ancient of Days [the Father], and they brought Him near before Him. Then to Him was given dominion and glory and a kingdom, that all peoples, nations...should serve Him. His dominion is an everlasting dominion... (Daniel 7:13-14).

By using this title "Son of Man," Jesus Christ emphasized two truths—that *He was fully God and fully human.* He is the God-man. He is the only One who is God that can draw so near on a heavenly cloud to the Ancient of Days (the Father's throne). Jesus was saying, "I am fully God yet fully human." I am God and I am also one of you.[9]

It may take a while before these truths connect and explode on the inside. I encourage you to study, gaze, and reflect on these truths. I pray it causes you to ponder the infinite truths of Jesus.

In his article *Disputation on the Divinity and Humanity of Christ,* Martin Luther expounds, "That in Christ there is a divine and a human nature, and these two natures in one person, so that they are joined together like no other thing, and yet so that humanity is not divinity, nor the divinity humanity, because that distinction in no way hinders but rather confirms the union...Christ is true God and true man."[10]

We do not say that Christ is merely a creature, but that he is God and man in one person. The natures are joined personally in the unity of the person. There are not two sons, not two judges, not two persons, not two Jesuses, but because of the undivided union and the unity of the two natures there is a communication of attributes, so that what is attributed to one nature is attributed to the other as well, because they are one person.[11]

Many men have pondered this fascinating truth. Nicholas of Cusa, in his writings *The Vision of God,* says, "For you are Creator and likewise creature, the Attracting and likewise the attracted, the Infinite and likewise the finite."[12]

> *Let this mind be in you which was also in Christ Jesus, who, being in the form of God, did not consider it robbery to be equal with God, but made Himself of no reputation, taking the form of a bondservant, and coming in the likeness of men. And being found in appearance as a man, He humbled Himself and became obedient to the point of death, even the death of the cross* (Philippians 2:5-8).

There is no one like Jesus Christ. In heaven, nor on earth, nor in the entire universe is there anyone like Him. Jesus Christ is fully God and fully man. He stands alone holding both dispositions, yet one.

Jesus is divinely God, with the divine nature, there was no time He was created or didn't exist. He was there from before time!

Jesus also was of human nature; He was the ideal man, the full embodiment that God intended God to be. Another way to say it is the Father and the Spirit are not human and no human being will ever be God. Jesus is the only One.

The reason why God had to become man was to reconcile heaven and earth. Psalm 115:16 says the heaven belongs to the Lord, but He gave the authority to man. To redeem humanity and the earth, there was no one who was qualified. The plan to redeem humankind was for God to become a man to reconcile heaven and earth as God intended.

Why is this so important for us to understand? Christ became the Son of Man that we might become the children of God. He took upon Himself our human nature that we might be *partakers of the divine nature* to commune with Him. If we can't partake of His divine nature, we can't commune with Him. The whole point of creation was to commune with Him. You are His eternal companion, because He wrapped Himself in the garments of humanity and was crushed by the wrath of God because of His commitment and His longing for you.

Our new self is of a completely different identity when we are new creatures in Christ. Isn't this so amazing? *"Therefore, if anyone is in Christ, he is a new creation; old things have passed away; behold, all things have become new"* (2 Cor. 5:17). We were the descendants of Adam, but now we are part of a new race descended from Christ Jesus. That is why this is so important to know. We are therefore *"partakers of the divine nature"* (2 Peter 1:4).

What we know about God is the most important thing because it's the most important thing about us. Knowing the God-Man Jesus is very significant to our hearts and lives. I pray that this chapter attracts you to search both intellectually and experientially this God-Man Jesus.

Jesus has so much passion for us; it is more than our human minds could ever comprehend. He gave His own life thinking of us the whole time, full of longing to have us near Him. Jesus' love and desire for us is infinite in measure and eternal in duration. He always loves effortlessly and in fullness. He never grows nor diminishes in love when He gives it away. It is sustained forever with intensity. His love is like a volcanic explosion of holy desire.

We were created in God's likeness for the purpose of relating to God. God designed the human spirit for partnership with Himself because He had plans to share so much with us forever. Salvation is so much more than escaping from hell, often referred to as "fire insurance." We are called to a relationship with Jesus forever in sharing His heart, being near Him, and doing the Father's work. Jesus wants people to be awestruck at His transcendent power and majesty and to participate in His transcendent love forever.

The privileges we hold as followers of Jesus far outweigh the privilege the disciples held in being able to walk with Him in person. We have the great revealer living within us, who will lead us right to Jesus.

We have not really known Jesus in our minds and we can barely comprehend the great mystery of the eternal divinity and His forever-human frame. Yet this Man whom we can know proves time and again of His great desire and love for us, not just in the laying down of His life but also in what He lives for today; He lives to make intercession for us at this very moment (see Heb. 7:25).

Jesus' desire is to make us feel loved and that we would celebrate our dignity and value. That is the main reason why He became a man, to redeem humankind. He finds pleasure in us, in sharing His heart with us, and in relating to us. He wants to partner with us in the work that His Father has entrusted to Him.

What we do matters in our interaction with God. Our actions move His heart. Our love for Him has a real impact on Him. He delights in our personality, our gifts, callings, and uniqueness. I can testify that many times I have felt and known that I moved His heart. I want to encourage you today that you move His heart all of the time.

In closing, I want to share two things that I hope will invite you into communion with this God-Man Jesus. Brother Lawrence shares his thoughts about Jesus, from his personal journey with Him:

> This King, who is full of goodness and mercy, doesn't punish me. Rather, He embraces me lovingly and invites me to eat at His table. He serves me Himself and gives me the keys to His treasury, treating me as His favorite. He converses with me without mentioning either my sins or His forgiveness. My former habits are seemingly forgotten. Although I beg Him to do whatever He wishes with me, He does nothing but caress me. This is what being in His holy presence is like.[13]

Last, I declare from the deepest part of who I am, that I love Jesus. I also acknowledge that I hardly know Him at all. But I love Him. Do you feel that way? I love Him but I just don't know Him in comparison to what there is to know. As I grow in the knowledge of Him, the more I want to know Him. We will spend all of eternity with Him—we get a long time to get to know each other. But I want to know Him right now. If that stirs and moves your heart, I want to charge you with this: get to know Jesus today, learn of the Man of whom you will be with for eternity.

Chapter 7

THE INDWELLING GOD

We need never shout across the spaces to an
absent God. He is nearer than our own soul,
closer than our most secret thoughts.
—A.W. Tozer, *The Pursuit of God*

The most glorious reality we get to experience is God Himself. Yes, I said experience, not just comprehend with our intellect. We have the capacity and the invitation to experience and commune with the Creator of the universe. The tragedy is very few people take the opportunity to commune and walk with God. Some, I would say, walk as Christian atheists; believing in God, but living as though He's not there. "Christian atheism" can be played out in a person's life in many ways, but primarily by disconnecting with the third person of the Trinity living inside them.

My goal is not just to make you aware of what we are not doing, but to also invite and inspire you to partake of the most glorious way to live: *communing with God Himself!*

If we get to commune with God, the question you may be asking is, how? How do we fellowship or commune with God? The answer is through the promised Holy Spirit, the third person of the Godhead.

The Holy Spirit is who we commune with day to day and hour by hour. He is the One we speak to, listen to, are directed by, follow, and enjoy. He is the means by which we partake of all the glorious attributes of having a relationship with the Creator God living inside us.

My hunch is that you have some knowledge of the Holy Spirit. Knowing this, I invite you to honestly reflect and ask yourself, *When was the last time I talked to Him? When was the last time I asked Him for direction in a decision, heard from Him or felt His presence? When was the last time I felt conviction or asked Him to help me walk out of sin? When was the last time I heard such powerful preaching that I felt His weighty presence? When was the last time I sat in quietness and heard His voice so audibly, I was undone for the rest of my day, or how about for the rest of my life?* Shouldn't this be our reality if the third Person of the Trinity lives inside of us and we commune with Him? Is communing with God a reality in your life? I present these questions, not to condemn, but to provoke us to greater intimacy than we currently experience.

VIEW OF GOD

After traveling to hundreds of cities around the world, I have seen many believers rally around the name of Jesus, but not many gather around the name of the Holy Spirit. Allen Hood spoke at our annual Pursuit Conference and relayed his thoughts on the view many have of the Holy Spirit in the Church today through his teaching, *Baptism of Holy Spirit and Fire.* "People treat the Holy Spirit as if He were their drunk uncle at the party. They keep Him in the back room, no one wants to let Him out, for fear of what He might say and do"[1]

This statement by Allen Hood is so true; we are uncomfortable with what we do not know. The Holy Spirit is the ultimate Pursuer. He's pursuing you right now. He wants to saturate your mind, will, and emotions. He wants to cause every cell of your being to love Christ Jesus. The Holy Spirit wants to take you on a guided tour from the inside out. He is your Guide (see John 16:13), your Helper (see John 14:16) and overflowing River of Life inside you (see John 7:38). He is your Eternal Companion. The same power that resurrected Jesus from the grave is the same power and Person who lives inside you right now (see Rom. 8:11). His name is Holy Spirit.

THE HOLY SPIRIT

The Holy Spirit is a great mystery. Our hearts yearn to know Him and we have the greatest invitation. Who is this Spirit of God with whom we can fellowship? Let's begin to understand who He is by looking at His name. His name is *Holy Spirit.* He is holy—we will discuss the significance of His holiness later on—and most importantly, He is spirit.

Let's begin by looking at the overall term of "spirit." I'm not talking about the Holy Spirit-God, but the substance of spirit. He is a spirit being. We know there is a spirit world that we do not see and that there are spirits. We also know there is a material world that we see. In his book *Life in the Spirit,* A.W. Tozer concludes that a "spirit is a specific and identifiable substance. If not definable, it can at least be described. Spirit is as real as matter, but it is another mode of being than matter."[2]

Matter and substance, however, are all around us. God made us from this matter, dirt from the ground; He made us and formed us from the earth's substance. That is why when we die, our physical bodies will return to the ground, back to the dirt (see Eccl. 12:7).

"Matter is one mode of being; spirit is another mode of being, as authentic as matter."[3] Material things are evident and visible to us. For example, matter has both mass and volume (occupies space). You can usually hold it, move it, and it is often solid. Even if it's a jelly form, it has an outline and can be moved. For example, water is a substance that can be moved from one place to another. Property and matter have specific elements and are part of the material world.

One power of the spirit, of any spirit (for I am talking about spirit now, not about the Holy Spirit), is its ability to penetrate. Matter bumps against other matter and stops; it cannot penetrate. Spirit can penetrate everything. For instance, your body is made of matter, and yet your spirit has penetrated your body completely. Spirit can penetrate spirit. It can penetrate personality—Oh, if God's people could only learn that spirit can penetrate personality that your personality is not an impenetrable substance, but can be penetrated.[4]

It's critical for us to understand this. Too many of us are focused on temporal, physical things that we see and not on the true existence of what we do not see. The spirit world is more real than what we see, taste, feel, smell, and hear. To some extent we understand this because God has placed eternity in our hearts, so we have a longing for the eternal (see Eccl. 3:11). It's also important to understand this because sin has taken the eyes of our understanding and has blinded us of this truth. Our spiritual eyes sense something, they see, even if dim. We instinctively know that there is a spiritual, unseen world, and we also know there is a God who is Spirit. So if we know there is God who is a Spirit being, *what is He?*

Now, what is the Holy Spirit? Not who, but what? The answer is that the Holy Spirit is a Being dwelling in another mode of existence. He has not weight, nor measure, nor size, nor any color, no extension in space, but He nevertheless exists as surely as you exist.[5]

WHO IS HE?

A.W. Tozer says it perfectly, describing Holy Spirit:

He is a person. Put that down in capital letters—that the Holy Spirit is not only a Being having another mode of existence, but

He is Himself a Person, with all the qualities and powers of personality. He is not matter, but He is substance. The Holy Spirit is often thought of as a beneficent wind that blows across the church. If you think of the Holy Spirit as being literally a wind, a breath, then you think of Him as nonpersonal and nonindividual. But the Holy Spirit has will and intelligence and feeling and knowledge and sympathy and ability to love and see and think and hear and speak and desire the same as any person has.[6]

Holy Spirit is a Person full of emotion, will, and great power; creative power that gives life. He is God. He is a Person. This is still argued upon. He is not an attribute of the Father and the Son. The Holy Spirit is God. Let's never confuse or minimize this truth as we talk about His being and personality. He is the third Person of the Trinity, and He is the consuming, majestic, all-powerful and all-knowing God!

HOLY SPIRIT'S QUALITIES AS A PERSON

Jesus introduced us to the Holy Spirit, and when He did, He gave some descriptions of who and what He does. He was there from creation hovering over the earth and created everything we see. The following are some qualities of the Holy Spirit:

- He has a mind—Romans 8:27

- He has a will—1 Corinthians 12:11

- He has emotions—Romans 15:30

- He speaks—Acts 13:2

- He bears witness and testifies—John 15:26, Romans 8:16

- He instructs—Nehemiah 9:20

- He prays and makes intercession—Romans 8:26

- He can be grieved—Ephesians 4:30

- He can be insulted—Hebrews 10:29

- He can be lied to—Acts 5:3

- He can be blasphemed—Matthew 12:31-32

- He can be resisted—Acts 7:51

- He can be quenched—1 Thessalonians 5:19

SYMBOLS AND WAYS HE REVEALS HIMSELF

All throughout Scripture we have seen God move. In some of those ways, He revealed Himself and showed some of His attributes. When the Holy Spirit hovered, He waited until the Word was spoken to create. From the very beginning we see Him as a life-giving Creator. I have seen Him move in various ways in my own life. Sometimes with great kindness and love, where all I could do was weep in His presence. Other times, He brought conviction to my heart that led me to repent and turn my heart toward Him. This is a great gift and what I consider to be the kindness of God that leads to repentance.

Here are other ways we have seen Him reveal Himself. These can also be symbols of Holy Spirit.

- *Water*—John 7:38-39; Isaiah 44:3

- *Fire*—Matthew 3:11; Isaiah 4:4; Acts 2:3

- *Wind or Breath*—Acts 2:2; John 3:8; Job 32:8

- *As a Dove*—Matthew 3:16; Luke 3:22

- *Oil*—Psalm 23:5; Psalm 92:10; Luke 4:18; Acts 10:38

- *Seal*—Ephesians 1:13

Allow me to define these a little more...

Water: The Spirit symbolized as water speaks of the life-giving flow, which refreshes, renews, and satisfies.

Fire: Fire symbolizes the holiness of God and the work of the Holy Spirit burning out all the hay, wood, and stubble of sin and compromise in our lives. The Spirit of Burning will not only purge, purify, and remove all the dross from our lives, but also sets our hearts ablaze with the zeal of the Lord to serve Him.

Wind and Breath: The symbol of wind represents renewal and inspiration of life. Wind is an invisible force outside of human control, but the wind controls many changes and patterns of seasons, both in the natural and in the spirit realm. Without breath there is no ability to speak, therefore the Spirit is the very essence behind God's ability to speak!

Dove: This symbolizes innocence, purity, and loyalty. Noah's dove found rest because the floodwaters of judgment had receded (see Gen. 8:8-12). At Jesus' baptism, the dove symbolized God's presence and anointing of Jesus as it "remained" or "abided" upon Him (see Matt. 3:16). This theme represents God's favor, approval, and faithfulness to us.

Oil: This represents the anointing abilities of the Holy Spirit who calls, equips, gifts, and enables believers to function in their ministry within the body of Christ.

Seal: The Holy Spirit is called the seal of "the purchased possession" (see Eph. 1:13), which is us, and refers to the Holy Spirit's declaration over our lives at salvation that we are God's, and promises God's inheritance to us. We are "marked" as God's for God's glory. I'm so thankful for this. We are His marked possession!

COMMUNE WITH HIM

...the communion of the Holy Spirit be with you all
(2 Corinthians 13:14).

The main purpose of this book is to inspire and invite you to be a partaker of God's divine nature through fellowship with God. One of the ways we get to partake of God's divine nature is through interacting and communing with the Holy Spirit. We must deeply value our relationship with the Holy Spirit. In Second Corinthians, Paul is exhorting the whole Corinthian church to commune with the Holy Spirit: *"the communion of the Holy Spirit be with you all"* (2 Cor. 13:14). This is God's invitation to all believers.

I see many Christians waiting to get into heaven to be close to God, to commune with Him and to know Him. I want to challenge this thinking for a second. There are many books out right now on heaven. There is a craze and a hunger to know what heaven looks like. I think it's great to get our focus off of the temporal and get our perspective from heaven. I think this will only increase as God is drawing our attention this way.

However, if you were transferred into heaven right now, you wouldn't be any closer to God than you are right now, because God is literally already here. Let that sink in for a bit. If you have given your life to God, then you have been made new by His Spirit and you have God living inside your being. God deposited into your spirit the seed of His very being. The eternal uncreated life of God came to live in you. You can't get any closer than that. He's literally inside your being right now. Yes, it's true. Think about that. God lives inside you right now.

HOW TO KNOW HIM

I just returned from the Philippines where I asked a group of business people a series of questions. I can still see the confused looks on their faces as I asked each question. But with every answer their eyes looked brighter.

I asked them: who is the Holy Spirit like? The answer: He is like Jesus. Then I asked, so who is Jesus like? The answer: He is just like the Father. You can know God right now by knowing the Holy Spirit for yourself! You can know the Father by knowing Jesus. You can know the Godhead through the Word and the Spirit. I want to invite you through this chapter to take hold of the greatest gift that Jesus said we could have—the Holy Spirit.

> *But this He spoke concerning the Spirit, whom those believing in Him would receive; for the Holy Spirit was not yet given, because Jesus was not yet glorified* (John 7:39).

Think about that for a moment. The Holy Spirit was not given or sent until Jesus was glorified. Remember that He comes upon those because Jesus is glorified first. He will never downpour and overflow into the life of any person except that the person glorifies Jesus. If Jesus is lifted up, He draws people to Himself (see John 12:32). The Holy Spirit becomes the great Pursuer; He will seek to know you, reveal truth to you, fill you, and show His favor upon your life. The grace of God comes upon your life and strengthens you! What an amazing promise, and what an amazing way to live.

Our Quest for Vibrancy

A vibrant walk with the Spirit is essential in our quest to experience God. It is futile to seek deep experiences with God while neglecting the Spirit's presence and leadership in our interior life.

We walk in the Spirit to the degree that we "fellowship with Him." The Spirit is a dynamic Person who lives inside us to empower our hearts as we walk in fellowship with Him. To fellowship with the Holy Spirit means we talk often to Him as we yield our heart to Him. It means we hear back from Him and have a two-way dialogue. Beloved, this is the greatest way to live. There is no other way to live! And this life is available to all if you surrender your life to Jesus!

The Holy Spirit honors our part in the relationship by not forcing us to dialogue with Him, if we choose not to. He does not want conversation or friendship with anyone who is not desperate or hungry for it.

Love requires a voluntary response. He waits, beckoning us to a deeper and more continual conversation.

WALKING TOGETHER

Can two walk together, unless they are agreed? (Amos 3:3)

I just love this verse in Amos 3:3. Walking together signifies not only walking as friends and being in agreement, but has the potential to be walking as one in some way.

I have worked with many churches in citywide events for almost a decade. Many church leaders work together by focusing on the things that they agree on and moving forward to advance the kingdom in unity.

Also, in marriage we can view our relationships as two people working things out to live harmoniously and working toward greater levels of mutual agreement.

> *But he who is joined to the Lord is one spirit with Him*
> (1 Corinthians 6:17).

God never wanted merely mutual agreement. He didn't want to be a far-off God, nor did He simply want to be near you. He wanted to be as close to you and me as possible, walking with us all the time. This is two becoming one, walking together in and toward greater and greater agreement.

I don't know about you, but I am hungry for this kind of relationship. This is how you and I were made. We were made to have communion with the third Person of the Trinity. We were made to know His heart, His secrets, in communion and partnership.

MADE IN HIS IMAGE

A very important task that I set out to accomplish in this book was to give a new perspective and a right view of God, even as I too am in pursuit of knowing Him. I believe we have barely scratched the surface. I also wanted to show how a right view of God is imperative to have a right view of ourselves. Therefore it's critical to know that we were made in His image and likeness. Why is this so important to note in this chapter? We are image bearers of the Godhead. We were made in His image.

> We read in Genesis, *"Then God said, 'Let Us make man in our image, according to our likeness"* (Gen. 1:26). It doesn't say, "I will make man in my image." No, it was the Father, Son, and the Holy Spirit creating man in unison. We are very aware of the Father and Son's role in Creation, but Scripture also clearly states, *"The Spirit of God has made me"* (Job 33:4), and again, *"You send forth Your Spirit, they are created"* (Ps. 104:30). So when God said, *"Let us make man in our image,"* the Holy Spirit was certainly included. We are created in the image of the Father, Son, and Holy Spirit.[7]

Now let's go back to discussing the Holy Spirit's name. We've discussed that He is a Spirit being, that He is a Person, and that we commune with Him. Now let's deal with the *Holy* part of His being.

HOLINESS AND THE INDWELLING GOD

And let them make Me a sanctuary, that I may dwell among them (Exodus 25:8).

As I stated previously, it's imperative for us to have a right view of God in order for us to have a right view of ourselves. This is also true concerning holiness. In order for us to commune with the Holy Spirit, we must understand that He is holy and He calls us to live holy: *"Be holy, for I am holy"* (1 Pet. 1:16). I want to take some time to explain this. It is essential in our walk with the Holy Spirit.

The tabernacle of Moses was the place where the presence of God dwelt and He wanted to be "among them." The whole reason we are called to be holy is because God is holy and He wants us near Him! Because God is holy, the place in which He dwells is holy too. It was for this very purpose that He instructed Moses to build a tabernacle so He could be among or with the people. He wanted this from the beginning. He wanted us close so when He calls us to greater levels of holiness, He is in essence calling us to greater levels of intimacy, or better said, closer to Him!

Many think that God wants us holy because He is mean and wants to place upon us rules and restrictions. The very opposite is true. He wants us holy because in the same way He desired a tabernacle to dwell among the people, He wants us holy so He can dwell with us in greater measure. In fact, the more we foster the presence of God and walk in step with the Holy Spirit, the holier we will inevitably become. Let me explain.

Notice in the original tabernacle of Moses that, the nearer you got to His presence, the holier it was. Those who went there lived a certain way to get nearer to God; it was a privilege. Holiness is measured by nearness to God. The more we have of His true presence, the more holiness and intimacy we have.

Andrew Murray describes it like this:

> We have only so much holiness as we have of God Himself... among men there is a very close link between the character of a house and its occupants. When there is no obstacle to prevent it, the house unintentionally reflects the master's likeness. Holiness expresses not so much an attribute as the very being of God in His infinite perfection, and His house testifies to one truth: He is holy, that where He dwells He must have holiness, that His indwelling presence makes holy.[8]

As followers of Jesus we have a choice to make. Will you be an outer court Christian, inner court Christian, or Holy of Holies Christian? In a previous chapter, "Our Original Design," we saw this parallel described further. The invitation is there for all of us to be in the Holy of Holies, which is the most intimate place with our God.

The very Spirit of God within us, the Holy Spirit, reveals Him to us. As He reveals God to us it transforms our nature and we become purified as we listen and are transformed into what the Holy Spirit shows us. *"But if we walk in the light as He is in the light, we have fellowship with one another, and the blood of Jesus Christ His Son cleanses us from all sin"* (1 John 1:7).

Many Christians do not realize there are varying degrees of nearness to God's presence. This was true in Israel and it remains true today. Today our body is a temple of the Holy Spirit (see 1 Cor. 6:19). It is our calling as believers to prepare our temples for God. We cannot seek holiness in itself, we must look at God and set our hearts to love and obey Him, and we will become holy for He is holy.

> *I dwell in the high and holy place, with him who has a contrite and humble spirit...* (Isaiah 57:15).

To pursue God's holiness takes humility, and God promises to dwell with us when we seek after Him in this way. We cannot have holiness without God's presence, and we cannot have God's presence without holiness. In the same way, we cannot even begin to respond to His pursuit of us without humility and a heart that is contrite. When we come to the place where we seek the Lord, humility and holiness are refined and the result is an increase of His presence in our lives.

Holiness is not a bad word or something to be avoided; and as I have stated in my previous book, *Relentless Pursuit,* to desire holiness is to desire God—because that is who He is. The pursuit of holiness is the pursuit of God; they are one in the same.

We can come boldly to Him through the blood of Christ that sanctified us and commune with the Holy Spirit as we continue on this life journey of being sanctified, empowered by His great grace. We want to be a people wholly given to a total heart consecration so we can expand more and more in our knowledge and experience of His nearness.

HIS VOICE

I have taught many people about the subject of hearing God's voice while inviting them to speak and listen to God. I also teach on the gift of prophecy, giving simple and practical steps for people to learn to hear God's voice and build up the Church.

Often people are looking for the voice of God in an audible way, with their human ears. Even if I tell them that hearing the audible voice of God is rare, many expect God to speak through their human ears. God mostly speaks inwardly to the heart. This is so hard for so many that it takes them days, weeks, and even sometimes years, rarely, if ever, recognizing God's voice for themselves. I have seen so many struggle with this glorious reality of being a Christian—speaking to Creator God from the inside all of the time.

> *The LORD passed by, and a great and strong wind tore into the mountains...and after the wind an earthquake...and after the earthquake a fire, but the LORD was not in the fire* [wind or earthquake]; *and after the fire a still small voice. So it was, when Elijah heard it.... Suddenly a voice came to him, and said, "What are you doing here, Elijah?"* (1 Kings 19:11-13)

We are all looking for the extravagance of God, the majestic thunder of His power and voice. We want to hear His voice clearly and we think there should be little or no effort involved.

I've been asked this many times, *Why wouldn't God speak loudly and clearly to me,* isn't He God after all? Let me answer that by asking another question. Have you ever thought of the possibility that we could be so un-renewed that we wouldn't be able to hear Him if He was speaking? Remember, we were not created to live from the outside in but from the inside out. The way God speaks is by speaking Spirit to spirit. He speaks to our heart. I am in no way saying that God doesn't speak in an outside audible voice, for He has and does. What I am saying is that the way He speaks to us mostly is on the inside, Spirit to spirit. For some of us, this may take some getting used to.

There are no two voices alike. God's voice is so unique, so tender and so gentle, yet so powerful. His voice is unmistakable and incomparable. His voice is like the sound of mighty rushing waters (see Rev. 1:15) and yet is also that still small voice (see 1 Kings 19:13).

PRACTICAL KEYS TO FELLOWSHIP WITH HIM

I want to take some time in the following section to give you some practical keys on how to fellowship with Him. Many wonder how to *walk* with the Holy Spirit, but it is as simple as *talking* with the Spirit. The fundamental way to walk in the Spirit is by maintaining an active dialogue with the indwelling Spirit. It is so simple that many miss it.

To get started, *I suggest talking directly to the Spirit several times a day for 3-5 minutes each time.*

If we just talk to Him, He will talk back! He will speak to us once He gets us in the conversation. He speaks to us by giving us subtle impressions that release power on our mind and heart if we respond to them. He will lead us by giving us promptings to act on.

We talk to the Spirit as a way to experience the release of His power in our inner self. The moments that we dialogue with Him are the moments we are most aware of His power in us.

He releases small measures of power on our mind and heart as we talk to Him, and the power is real. We experience the Spirit's power in small incremental ways like we do with food and water. Over time we can look back and see the evidence of His increased power in our lives.

We must cultivate our friendship with the Spirit, being careful not to quench or resist Him. Paul exhorted us to not quench (see 1 Thess. 5:19) or grieve the Spirit (see Eph. 4:30). Therefore, we must prize, watch, and guard the prompting of the Spirit on our heart. We must renounce all that causes the Holy Spirit's work in our heart to be minimized (see Gal. 6:8; Rom. 8:6). We can grow in our experience of the indwelling Holy Spirit. As we talk to Him and He talks back, we will grow.

> As we linger in His presence, speak affectionately, speak slowly, softly (not shouting at the indwelling Spirit), briefly (short phrases not paragraphs, even reducing phrases to one word) and minimally (listen twice as much as talking by limiting our speaking to one third) with many pauses, praying with our spirit (1 Cor. 14:2) along with gently sighing (Rom. 8:26) with gazing in silence for few seconds or minutes. "Less is more" in terms of amount and volume of speaking.[9]

BEGIN NOW

Begin right now! Commune with the Holy Spirit; He is wooing you, beckoning you, and drawing you to Him. His voice is clear and His presence sweet. His love is strong and His eyes are set on you. All we have to do is begin to dialogue with Him.

I remember the first times that I began to realize that He was there when I began to speak to Him. It is really this simple. I could sense His presence. I now am able to hear, sense, change, and much more—all from communing with Him. Begin by saying, *"I honor Your presence in my life, Holy Spirit. I love You, Holy Spirit. I welcome You to increase in my life."* Whether you have an active relationship with the Holy Spirit or this is new for you, start today and watch your heart come alive as you learn to commune on the inside with this great gift God has given.

Enjoy!

Chapter 8

THEATER OF WAR

There is a war going on, and your
mind is the battlefield.
—Joyce Meyer, *Battlefield of the Mind*

I arrived home from work one day in 1998 nearly one year after Christelle and I got married. Christelle was in an unusually cheerful mood. She was glowing, her beautiful smile lit up her face, and her eyes were sparkling. She was evidently excited about something as if it were a special occasion. If it was a special occasion, I didn't remember. What was even worse, I didn't get any of her carefully prepared clues she was giving. When I sat down as usual for dinner, I noticed she had arranged a very nice meal. She had prepared baby peas, baby carrots, and baby back ribs for dinner. She called special attention to the name of each item on the plate.

Honestly, I was hungry. The growls erupting in my stomach consumed my thoughts, not noticing that she was excitedly waiting for me to "get it." Sitting across from me, smiling and realizing I still had no idea, she reached under the table and proceeded to pull out a card and present wrapped in baby paper. I stopped eating, feeling a bit puzzled as to what this was all about. I opened the card and my heart stopped as I read the words, "We are having a baby, congratulations, Daddy!" My thoughts seemed to move in slow motion, and I sat there stunned as the realization that I was going to be a father hit me.

We were so excited that we immediately wrapped up the food, and I called my parents, brothers, and sister and promptly arranged to meet them at a restaurant to share with them and celebrate our exciting news. What a celebration we had! I was ecstatic! Reality hadn't set in yet, but my heart was overjoyed. After the party we made our phone calls to share the exciting news with friends and family. That night I laid in bed staring into the darkness thinking about the new life coming and the reality of my life up to this point. We were becoming a family with this new baby coming. I began to search my heart, and I knew I wanted so much more.

I was not on fire for God to say the least. I wouldn't even say I was living a hypocritical life. Admittedly I was living a fully secular life, separated from God, which did not mirror my core values and what I grew up knowing a Christian life to be like. The spiritual condition of my heart at this point was at the lowest, driest point I have ever experienced. Dutifully, we attended church most Sundays, but I knew better and had experienced much more of God throughout my life already. When I was between 14 and 16 years of age, I had experienced radical, real encounters with God in my interior life. I had spoken to God, and I had heard from Him. I read the Bible for hours as my source of entertainment. I had times of real joy, filled with tears and real God encounters, but not anymore. Those times with God seemed to be nothing but distant memories.

This new reality of where my heart was, was brought on by the thoughts of the new baby coming—and it was shaking me on the inside. In my heart, a new desire arose to have God be the center of my life, and I knew that the wisdom to lead a family could only be found in Him. And strangely while lying there, I began to feel led by the Lord to watch our wedding video.

I walked to the living room and inserted the video. As I sat on the couch in the middle of the night watching our wedding video, I began to feel that sweet familiar presence of the Holy Spirit come into the room. It had been so long, I was so dry, and the realization that He wanted me and was waiting for me touched my heart—now I was feeling Him once again.

Being faced with my barrenness, I was like a dry sponge in His presence as I soaked in His nearness; I wanted desperately to get right with Him. I knew from past experience that when I am in Him, it is only then that things are right, that I am satisfied, that I am whole; it is only in Him that I really live. With tears flowing down my face, on my knees, in front of the television set, I cried out to God, "God help me. I don't know what to do. I have sinned against You and walked away from You. Forgive me. Wash me and restore my life." As I got up from the floor that night, I knew He washed me from sin and compromise. Now, I needed His help. I didn't know what to do, but I had a willing heart that said, "Yes" to whatever He wanted.

A few days later the help came to me. I went to church that day. Living Word Christian Center, in Brooklyn Park, Minnesota. The pastor was speaking, and truthfully I didn't understand much of what he said. There was, however, one thing I did hear; during the offering those who were attending the church for the first time were invited to complete an information card, and upon receipt of the card the previous week's teaching tape would be given as a free gift.

The next day I had a 45-minute drive, so I listened to the tape. The subject was on "renewing your mind" through the Word of God. As the pastor began to teach, the truths of what he was speaking began to really impact my heart. He gave insights about the power of the Word of God, that it is *"living and active"* (Heb. 4:12) and literally as he was saying these things I could feel the life; it was penetrating my heart. The Holy Spirit was awakening me and as the Word of God was spoken, revelation was coming and my eyes were being opened.

This was the beginning of the answer I was looking for. I wanted help, and I wanted to know how to be a good husband and a good father. I wanted to lead a great family one day. God sent me the plan; He gave me the answer: *get in the Word of God, renew your mind.* The solution was to change my thinking that can only be done through the Word of God.

THEATER OF WAR

In this chapter I will discuss one of the keys to having vibrancy in your interior life. There is a massive war of the greatest proportions happening in the members of our soul and it is in the arena of our mind. It seems like World War III, but the good news is that God is on your side and you can walk in victory!

> *Dear friends, I urge you, as foreigners and exiles, to abstain from sinful desires, which wage war against your soul* (1 Peter 2:11 NIV).

Peter is urging us here to have a higher vision. First he calls us *"foreigners and exiles."* Another Bible version calls us *"pilgrims."* We are heaven-bound. Therefore, with this viewpoint and focus God calls us to separate ourselves and abstain from sinful desires that are at war against our mind, will, and emotions. We have real enemies that attack our peace, joy, and our communion with God.

Let's take a look at the war going on in our thoughts. I want to give the solution and some practical steps to living a life where we are being transformed, going from glory to glory, walking by great faith and communing with God like never before in our lives!

The Mind is the Forerunner of Your Life

For as he thinks in his heart, so is he (Proverbs 23:7).

The mind is the leader or forerunner of all actions. Proverbs 23:7 describes the powerful influence thoughts have on how you live and who you become. Many people's problems, or sin issues, are rooted in thinking patterns that actually produce problems that they will experience in their lives. The devil begins by bombarding our mind with a cleverly devised pattern of little nagging thoughts, suspicions, doubts, fears, wonderings, reasonings, and theories. He studies us patiently and finds our weak points, vulnerabilities, and areas void of or lacking truth. He knows what we like and don't like. He knows our insecurities, weaknesses, and our fears. If we don't get a handle on the way we think, someone or something else will. I am not talking about just barely coping in the arena of our mind, but I want to give you vision for the victorious life in the mind, which is the theater of war.

> I wholeheartedly believe our thoughts lead us, charting the course for our lives and pointing us in certain directions that ultimately determine our destinations in life. Our thoughts cause us to have certain attitudes and perspectives; they affect our relationships; they determine how productive we will be personally and professionally; and they greatly influence the overall quality of our lives. We absolutely must understand the power of thoughts.[1]

The majority of circumstances in our lives really grow out of the thoughts that we think—both good and bad. We often think that we fall subject to the circumstances that come to us, when most of the time it is actually quite the opposite. While it remains true that some circumstances are out of our control, most of the circumstances we find ourselves in can be attributed to and are a direct result of our thinking. Taking control of our thoughts is powerful and can alter our circumstances and change our emotions. Thoughts create desires and attitudes that are secretly fostered in the mind, and then opportunity arises and actions are executed to bring forth the culmination of our thoughts. The course of our life is created through our thoughts. "Circumstance does not make the man; it reveals him to himself."[2] "Men do not attract that which they want, but that which they are."[3]

In *Mind is the Master,* James Allen, philosopher of the human spirit, writes:

> The soul attracts that which it secretly harbors; that which it loves, and also that which if fears; it reaches the height of its cherished aspirations; it falls to the level of its unchastened desires and circumstances are the means by which the soul received its own. Every thought seed sown or allowed to fall into the mind, and to take root there, produces its own, blossoming sooner or later into act, and bearing its own fruitage of opportunity and circumstance. Good thoughts bear good fruit, bad thoughts bad fruit.[4]

So as you can see, the mind is the starting point for a person's life, both good and bad. Sustained thoughts or thinking patterns will inevitably produce a person's character and circumstances. Even if a person cannot always choose their circumstances, they can choose their thoughts and thereby indirectly shape and influence their circumstances. So, the mind is the starting point for a person's life. God created the mind to be one of the most powerful agents in leading and directing our path. Loving God and communing with God is so connected with understanding our thoughts and our mind that we must begin here in order to produce the life we all desire.

LOVING GOD WITH ALL YOUR MIND

You shall love the LORD your God...with all your mind...
(Mark 12:30).

God created us in His own image and likeness as revealed in Genesis 1:26. One aspect of this is seen in the complexity of the human mind. It is like a mysterious, internal universe with a memory more powerful than a computer with trillions of gigabytes. We don't fully understand the vastness of our mind with all its intricacies, imaginations, and creativity, and the purpose it serves in unifying our emotions and attitudes, helping to create good and bad habits.

The arena of our mind is critical. Whatever stirs our mind directly impacts our mood and emotions. Our emotions so much of the time affect our decision-making. We think and say way too often that we "don't feel like it" or we "don't want to." The impact that our own mind and thoughts have upon our life and our actions is astounding. What we are motivated to do is from the thoughts we think and the way we think as a lifestyle. Our mind gets empowered into the ways of God the very same way it gets pulled into sin. Fill your mind with God, with thoughts of Him, and watch your motivations change as you get addicted to Him.

The language of the mind is images. It is an internal movie screen that provides us with pictures. Our memory is a vast reservoir of near endless visuals. Imagination was powerfully given to us by God to visualize His truth and to interact with Him in a deep and continual way throughout eternity.

We are constantly in a movie and having conversation in our mind. The Lord created us this way for ceaseless dialogue with Him. So much of our life is lived in our minds, because we can never turn our minds off. It is the continual reality and stream of our life. When our body sleeps, our mind stays active, dreaming through the night.

Our mind defines so much of who we are and how we love. We can express ourselves in many ways, but still only a very small percentage of what we think can be expressed and known.[5]

How do we really love God with all of our mind? I take this to mean that we direct our thinking in a certain way—toward God. Our thinking should be completely engaged to do all it can to express thoughts that honor God, that cultivate love for Him and those around us. This includes to intentionally *"set your mind on things above, not on things on the earth"* (Col. 3:2). Setting our minds on loving God includes removing the wrong mindset that diminishes our love, such as shame, bitterness, lust, and ingratitude, and filling our minds with truth. We will discuss this more a little bit later.

God is inviting and commanding us to love Him with all of our mind. So why is loving God and the way we think connected? "The main reason that thinking and loving are connected is that we cannot love God without knowing God; and the way we know God is by the Spirit-enabled use of our minds. So to 'love God with all your mind' means engaging all your powers of thoughts to know God as fully as possible in order to treasure Him for all He is worth."[6] This is within the grasp of every believer to reach for by the power of the Holy Spirit; but we have to set our minds, which means we have to be intentional about it.

RENEWED MIND

And do not be conformed to this world, but be transformed by the renewing of your mind, that you may prove what is that good and acceptable and perfect will of God (Romans 12:2).

Paul begins by telling us what not to do, *"do not be conformed to this world."* The warning not to conform is telling us not to pattern or fashion our life, character, or thoughts in accordance to the world's system. Paul is commanding us not to imitate the way the world lives. Then Paul tells us what we are to do to avoid conforming to the pattern of the world, and that is by *renewing our minds.* If we want to change or to go a different direction, then we must renew our minds.

This raises the question: Do you like the way your life is being played out in your relationships, combatting sin issues, addictions? Or if you feel stuck in some way and want to see change, there is only one way—renew your mind. You don't simply change your actions on the outside, you change what and how you think through renewing your mind. In other words, if your mind stays the same, your life stays the same; but if you renew your mind, then your life will be transformed from the inside out.

WHAT DO WE THINK ABOUT?

Being people who are healthy and whole in our minds is something everyone wants for their lives. We know that God has supplied the grace we need to combat the sin of destructive thinking, yet so much of the time we take casually the importance of thinking God's way. Unless stopped, wrong thinking over time increases until we believe full-blown lies; and these in turn become strongholds that deceive us every day. We see everything in life through this lens and it not just taints us but also eventually destroys us.

If we want to live full lives of vibrancy and joy, we must learn the truths of thinking God's way.

> *We demolish arguments and every pretension that sets itself*
> *up against the knowledge of God, and we take captive*

every thought to make it obedient to Christ (2 Corinthians 10:5 NIV).

There is a war inside, and it is in the arena of our minds. We must begin to recognize that it is not what is on the outside that is destroying, but what is going on in the inside of our thinking. The thoughts we allow to go through our minds form our thinking patterns, worldviews, and belief systems. If these thoughts do not come from the Word of God, we are in serious danger, even if we do not recognize it right away.

Our minds are like a train station. Our thoughts are like the multiple train cars going by. We can choose to get on and ride any one of those cars (thoughts) and allow them to take us wherever it is headed, or we can choose to let it pass by. The choice is completely ours. We can lead our thoughts—or we can let them lead us.

Thoughts contrary to Him are direct arguments to truth and bring us slowly but surely down a path of death.

We cannot treat our thoughts with casualness. These instructions from the Lord are not options to be considered, but commands to be obeyed. God does not want us living a life that is being tossed to and fro by our emotions. He wants us to be liberated and free from those lies and arguments that exalt themselves above our God.

THINK ON SUCH THINGS

Finally, brothers and sisters, whatever is true, whatever is noble, whatever is right, whatever is pure, whatever is lovely, whatever is admirable—if anything is excellent or praiseworthy—think about such things (Philippians 4:8 NIV).

This is one of the most profound passages and the clearest instructions to lead you into right thinking. In order to follow these instructions for right thinking, let's look at the words in this passage a little deeper.

My wife, Christelle, has an amazing teaching on what to think about according to Scripture. Let me share some of her insights.

Whatever is true: These instructions start with what is true because each point that follows is all truth, and are insights into how Jesus thinks, which is truthful in every way. Jesus is *"the way, the **truth**, and the life"* (John 14:6). Therefore whatever Jesus thinks, the Holy Spirit thinks and God the Father thinks is *truth.* "Let God be true but every man be a liar" (see Rom. 3:4). So the question to ask ourselves when a thought runs through our mind, *Is this what God thinks?* If it is not, then it is a lie and *an argument that sets itself up against the knowledge of God* (see 2 Cor. 10:5). These wrong thoughts or lies must be cast down. The ultimate test of truth is the Bible. If a thought you are thinking, or worse a *way* of thinking, does not line up with God's Word, it must be taken into captivity and thrown away. Every thought that we *think* must be weighed; and we cannot allow ourselves to indulge in that which is not truth. Ask yourself, *Is this what God thinks?* and find out by searching the Bible and talking to the Holy Spirit. We are in an age when believers have a grave Bible deficit, yet the Bible is more available than it has ever been. It is time to start eating truth and letting the truth set us free (see John 8:32). Become a truth lover.

Whatever is noble/honorable: These are the things that are worthy of honor or respect, those things that have true value. We are to admire, think on those traits and characteristics that are godly and admirable, that have value beyond this earth. The things that matter are those things we bring with us into eternity. Doing this will produce in itself honorable qualities.

Whatever is right: Thinking on things that are *right* is to think in agreement with God's perfect, unchanging standards as revealed in Scripture. To know what is right we must be students of the Word of God and have hearts that say yes to God in obedience. We cannot let things slide, even if we feel they are small or because we have always thought a certain way. We must violently line up our thinking and become conformed to the image of God by submitting to His righteousness and *right* thinking.

Whatever is pure: Thinking purely means to have undefiled thoughts. We are to especially focus on things that are free of immorality, greed, and sexual impurity. What we set our minds on either defiles or cleans. It is one or the other; we are never at a standstill. Impure thoughts defile us and poison the whole person. Purity in thought leads to purity in life.

Whatever is lovely: Things that are lovely are those thoughts about another that produce action that benefits the other person. We are to think on ways that benefit people. It is the opposite of vengeful, bitter, and action that produces fear and punishment of others. It is having an attitude of sympathy, compassion, longsuffering, and thoughts toward the well-being of others.

Whatever is admirable/good repute: We must focus on the things that are of good reputation and things well thought of. We are to refuse to believe an evil report of someone, and we are to focus on what we can think of and speak well of another.

Whatever is excellent: Paul is summing up here how to think. The first quality we are to add as believers to our life is moral excellence. We must determine to obey God and His commands. When we do not, our growth is hindered. This speaks of moral excellence that is *lived,* not just spoken of or thought. Believers demonstrate virtue and moral excellence by living how we should, therefore we are to think on ways to live as we should. We must think about how to walk out godliness in our lives and plan for it, by thinking about how to carry it out.

Worthy of praise: This means to literally give praise, approval, and express admiration to God. We are to think on godly actions that deserve this type of response. We need to ask ourselves, *Is this praiseworthy?* Then think and meditate on it. The qualities of God are the most praiseworthy thoughts to think. When we choose not to be critical of others, we give praise to God by seeing praiseworthy things in those around us.

Let your mind think about/dwell on: We are to actually take into account, reason, calculate, weigh, and deliberate. We are supposed to literally think about these things deliberately and in a logical and detailed way, using our reasoning and coming to conclusions, through careful study. We are to deliberately determine what to think as we would any other thing. We are to think on all these things in such a manner that we let them shape our life and conduct. It is very practical when we choose to dwell on these things; it will make us into who we are longing to be and what we want to feel. *To dwell on* is actually meditation, and the word in this passage is used in the present tense, which means we must do it regularly and continually.

Paul implies that we have the power to govern our thoughts and therefore are responsible for them. If the thoughts are governed well, the outward life will follow suit. Notice this is not the power of positive thinking that has become so popular. What the Bible teaches is to think and focus on is what is true according to God Himself. Thoughts based on Scripture are living and active inside us.

THE HABIT OF THINKING

Do not be deceived, God is not mocked; for whatever a man sows, that he will also reap. For he who sows to his flesh will of the flesh reap corruption, but he who sows to the Spirit will of the Spirit reap everlasting life (Galatians 6:7-8).

This is a principle that no one will argue: sowing and reaping. We know that when we sow seed into the ground it will bring forth a crop. Yet we rarely think about this principle when it comes to our thoughts. We can easily forget about sowing good seed and training our mind on a consistent basis to create a return on our thoughts.

Man is, in the nature of things, a being of habit, and this he cannot alter; but he can alter his habits. He cannot alter the law of his nature, but he can adapt his nature to the law.[7]

Habit is *repetition*. Man repeats the same thoughts, the same actions, the same experiences over and over again until they are incorporated with his being, until they are built into his character as part of himself….Man, today is the result of millions of repetitious thoughts and acts. He is not ready-made, he becomes, and is still becoming. His character is predetermined by his own choice. The thoughts, the act, which he chooses, that, by habit, he becomes.[8]

I am seeking to change my own life through changing my thoughts and renewing my mind. I am interested in loving God in a deep and tangible way, and that is created by new habits that will result in success.

Meditate for Life and Success

His delight is in the law of the Lord, and in His law he meditates day and night. He shall be like a tree planted by the rivers of water, that brings forth its fruit in its season, whose leaf also shall not wither; and whatever he does shall prosper (Psalm 1:2-3).

This is one of my favorite Scriptures for living a successful and prosperous life, which we all desire. Those who want to not just bring forth fruit, but bring it forth in season are being invited to meditate on the Word of God day and night. There are no shortcuts; there is no other way. This is the narrow road to prosperity of the body, soul, and spirit.

Prospering in life begins in *delighting* in the Word of God. This means to take pleasure and enjoyment in the Word of God. When you take pleasure in something, you think about it and you apply your energy and passion. When I take pleasure or enjoyment in something, I give my affections to it. This is one of the easiest ways to measure what I delight in.

One of the things I see and hear is how reading the Bible is boring and many times people fall asleep when they read the Scriptures. I want to invite you to see how one of the greatest men in history enjoyed the Scriptures. I share this to whet your appetite for what could be possible in your own life. Let me introduce you to Jonathan Edwards; he was a great theologian, intellectual, pastor, and one of the leaders in the first Great Awakening in the United States. He deeply loved the Scriptures. He said this:

> I had then, and at other times, the greatest delight in the Holy Scriptures, of any book whatsoever. Oftentimes in reading it, every word seemed to touch my heart. I felt a harmony between something in my heart, and those sweet and powerful words. I seemed often to see so much light exhibited by every sentence, and such a refreshing food communicated, that I could not get a long in reading; often dwelling long on one sentence, to see the wonders contained in it; and yet almost every sentence seemed to be full of wonders.[9]

If you are not delighting in the Word of God, I encourage you to take the next step...meditate on the Word of God.

Meditation on the Word of God can be defined as to "ponder by speaking to yourself." Our goal is to devour the Word of God by reading it again and again and thoughtfully meditating upon it, and then we are empowered and transformed. Meditation is an invitation to utter, speak, mutter—and an important word is to *imagine* the Word of God. Meditating is slow repetition in your mind, but most importantly out of your mouth. You must speak the Word. Meditating is a lost art of renewing the mind and cultivating the life of God on the inside.

My good friend Corey Russell wrote a powerful book titled *Ancient Paths*. It is one of the books our students in the Pursuit Internship are assigned to read. Corey speaks about rediscovering delight in the Word of God through meditation:

> When we enter into the slow repetition of meditation, one of the first barriers we encounter is overfamiliarity with the Scriptures. It takes time to unlearn a passage in order to experience the full glory of each verse. I have found that repetition is one of the greatest ways to break down overfamiliarity and create a new vulnerability in our spirits to the power of the Word. When we slow down and begin to speak back to God the things He has spoken to us, we increasingly realize how little we know. Repetition forces us to confront the hidden pride of our hearts and the desire to move on to something new and different, something that will expand our knowledge base swiftly and effortlessly. This is why we must have a vision for breakthrough in the Word of God; without this vision, we will lack the patience and perseverance needed to push past knowledge and into revelation.[10]

How do we live on the Word? We must "come to Jesus" in the Word. (See Matthew 4:4.)

There is a difference between studying the Bible and meditating on it. Let me show you three important points to help explain this.

First we must understand that we are to search the Scriptures—we must not underestimate the value of Bible study. Although life can be found through study, it is not in Bible study alone. We must not think that by just studying the Bible we will experience life. Life is experienced when we connect to the life of the Bible that is Jesus, who connects us to God's heart. I like to say *encountering the God between the lines*, Jesus the Word of God.

The second difference between study and meditation is that study focuses on the mind, and that's important. I don't want to minimize this in any way. We must not underestimate the value of diligently studying the Word of God. Unfortunately there is a great deficit of knowledge of the Bible, and in turn an even greater deficit of knowing who God really is; subsequently, God calls us to *rightly divide the Word of truth* (see 2 Tim. 2:15). The Word of God is the sword of the Spirit (see Eph. 6:17), which we are supposed to know and be able to use. We want to know the Bible and study it, to know the Man-Jesus.

Meditation, however, focuses on the heart. Meditation is essentially lifting our heart directly to the Lord Jesus. In the end, studying should always lead to meditation.

Meditation brings us into a devotional dialogue with Jesus. We should be after a living, affectionate conversation with a Man, an interaction with His heart. We don't have to be Bible theologians to experience the power of Jesus in this way.

Richard J. Foster defines what takes place in meditation:

> What happens in meditation is that we create the emotional and spiritual space which allows Christ to construct an inner sanctuary in the heart. The wonderful verse *"I stand at the door and knock..."* was originally penned for believers, not unbelievers (Rev. 3:20). We who have turned our lives over to Christ need to know how very much he longs to eat with us, to commune with us. He desires a perpetual Eucharistic feast in the inner sanctuary of the heart. Meditation opens the door and, although we are engaging in specific meditation exercises at specific times, the aim is to bring this living reality into all of life.[11]

TRUE LIFE FOUND

I encourage people to read the Bible one book at a time. I see a lot of life in reading a book of the Bible in its entirety, but the power of meditating on the Word of God can be done on one verse, several verses, or a whole portion. The Word of God is living and active (see Heb. 4:12). It will produce life in your heart if you let it. This is the greatest way you can walk and talk with God, through the living Word of God.

I want you to ponder this next verse for a minute. The Word of God has so much life and multiplying seed that God promises abundant life will spring forth as we declare and place the Word of God in our hearts. It will produce abundant fruit in our lives!

> For as the rain comes down, and the snow from heaven, and do not return there, but water the earth, and make it bring forth and bud, that it may give seed to the sower and bread to the eater, so shall My word be that goes forth from My mouth; it shall not return to Me void, but it shall accomplish what I please, and it shall prosper in the thing for which I sent it (Isaiah 55:10-11).

Life comes from knowing, studying, and meditating on the Word of God. Its takes delighting and meditating on the Word to bring forth the abundant life that it is meant to bring. So how do you really meditate on it, you might ask? Let me briefly share this story to give you some practical steps about how to meditate on the Word of God.

Shortly after God highlighted the power of His Word and began renewing my mind, He started giving me some practical things to do while I was at work or at school. I desperately wanted to renew my mind, and I was encountering the Man between the lines, Jesus. An abundant life was being produced inside me. I had new joy, peace, and revelation coming to me.

I felt the Lord inviting me to further encounter Him. He gave me an idea to write Scriptures on note cards. I had been reading the Bible, but He was inviting me to know the Word more intimately and to search out His heart and emotions through the Scriptures. I began to memorize and ponder various verses, one at a time. I would also talk about verses to Christelle and those around me, if they were open to it. But mostly I began to think about it and speak to God about it.

I still do much of this today, and I also love to ask God about the verse and ask Him for the Spirit of revelation to come. I ask Him questions like, "What are You saying to me about this verse? Why are You highlighting this verse to me?"

I encourage you to slow down and ponder what you are reading. Allow God to speak to you through the language of His Word. Say a phrase to God, memorize it, and cry out to God for the light of understanding to mark your heart. God is living understanding. Allow Him to reveal the Word to you. I like praying in tongues while reading a Bible verse before, during, and even afterward to allow the Holy Spirit to deposit truth and revelation deep within. Another very helpful thing to do is sing the Bible. Find verses or phrases straight from Scripture and make songs.

Doing these things will bring great revelation to the Bible and cause your heart to come alive. When there is no revelation knowledge of the Word, it is only head knowledge and not heart knowledge. God doesn't just want us to know the Bible through our intellect, He wants us to absorb and digest the Word of God until it marks our hearts, and then in turn our will and emotions come into alignment with the life of God.

COME TO HIM

You search the Scriptures, for in them you think you have eternal life; and these are they which testify of Me. But you are not willing to come to Me that you may have life (John 5:39-40).

What we are after in our lives is not head knowledge, but a life transformed by the Word of God, which only comes through revelation knowledge of the Word. The word "revelation" literally means, "to unveil," and that only occurs when the Holy Spirit takes the unsearchable things of God—previously hidden from humanity's understanding—and reveals them to us by His grace (see John 14-16; 2 Cor. 2:9-11).

We must get an understanding that we can't do this without the Holy Spirit. John 15:26 declares, *"But when the Helper comes, whom I shall send to you from the Father, the Spirit of truth who proceeds from the Father, He will testify of Me."* So we must rely on the Holy Spirit to give us understanding and reveal the Word (Jesus) to us.

In John 5:39-40 Jesus rebuked the Pharisees for searching the Scriptures to acquire head knowledge or intellect. Information about God doesn't take you into intimate knowledge of God. He is inviting us to seek Him in and through the Word to encounter Him and know Him. We must go to Him.

Let's look at some biblical figures who asked God to reveal Himself to their hearts. David asked God to "open his eyes" to His Word (see Ps. 119:18). Paul prayed for a spirit of revelation (see Eph. 1:17-19). Jesus exhorted the Laodicean church to anoint their eyes with eye salve to see (see Rev. 3:18). Psalm 119:18 declares, *"Open my eyes, that I may see wondrous things from Your law."*

Daniel, after studying the Scriptures diligently for decades, was given "skill to understand" what is noted in the "Scripture of Truth" (see Dan. 7:15-16; 8:16-17,19; 10:21). Why would God give us more insight if we neglect the treasure that He's already spoken in the Word?

And he [Gabriel] *informed me...and said, "O Daniel, I have now come forth to give you skill to understand..."* (Daniel 9:22).

God literally gives us the skill to understand the hidden truths in the Word by looking, meditating, and speaking to Him about His very own Word. It's literally God revealing God to us.

Transformed by Beholding

But we all, with unveiled face, beholding as in a mirror the glory of the Lord, are being transformed into the same image from glory to glory, just as by the Spirit of the Lord (2 Corinthians 3:18).

As I briefly mentioned in a previous chapter, there is a principle in Scripture called the "Beholding Becoming" principle. This is one of the most important aspects of renewing our mind. Beholding Becoming means that whatever we behold is what we become. The only way we are changed into His likeness is through the revelation of who God is, what He's like, how He feels, and what we look like to Him. It takes the unfolding of what God is really like to transform us into a new people, full of faith in who God really is and not what we think He's like.

As we fill our eyes, our ears, our minds, and our mouths with the things of God, we will in time become transformed into the same reality. Not only will our minds and thoughts be about Him, but also our very beings and character will look like His.

For example, if I want to grow in my revelation concerning the kindness of God, then I begin to highlight passages that speak about the kindness of God. I then begin to read these passages over and over, highlighting the phrases, praying the phrases, and speaking these phrases out. This is the simplest way to becoming like Him. This takes time, consistency, and a focus in pursuit of Jesus, the Man between the lines.

SUMMARY

In summary, we want to live from the inside out. There is no better way than to encounter God by meditating and transforming our minds through the Word of God. In essence we are encountering Jesus, the Word, the Man between the lines. This is divine pleasure when it hits our hearts. This is allowing the Spirit of God to lead our lives, our will and emotions through a life transformation. If we don't transform the way we think, we will come up short and the journey of communion won't last long. This is the way to live for life. It takes a daily posturing of our hearts, minds, and physical appetites—and making them obedient unto Christ!

Chapter 9

BREAKING FREE FROM A DULL HEART

*Keep your heart with all diligence, for
out of it spring the issues of life.*
—KING SOLOMON

Oftentimes we make commitments to keep our dreams alive. We go to conferences and read books to work on our marriages to help keep them vibrant and successful. We take stewardship classes on financial accountability to ensure we budget our finances and invest properly. We work, train, and invest in many things, but so often we fail to invest in keeping our hearts alive.

The heart is the seat of emotions, thoughts, hurts, sorrows, joys, memories; it is where all actions come from. If a person's heart is good, he or she will have a good life, for the issues of life flow from the heart.

The heart in the human body pumps blood that flows to the rest of the body. As long as the heart is alive, the body is living. Doctors go to great lengths to keep the heart alive in a state of emergency. The same is true of our heart spiritually speaking. We must also go to great lengths to sustain a heart that is alive. We must ensure that we keep our heart (mind, emotions, thoughts) clear and undefiled.

The Bible warns us in Proverbs 4:23 to *"Keep your heart with all diligence, for out of it spring the issues of life."* Solomon in his wisdom tells us that if we want to direct our lives properly, we must guard our heart.

To begin this chapter, I want to dive into the negative aspects or the warning signs of not keeping our hearts alive. Then we will create a plan to either awaken or posture our hearts to sustain a heart fully alive in Him. I believe this is one of the greatest needs of the hour in which we live. Too many Christians seem to be walking zombies doing what seems to be all the right stuff, yet all the while they are simply walking with dull and sleeping hearts. They are, in essence, "sleepwalking."

OUTWARD VITALITY, INWARD DECLINE

Tragically, we can have all the outward appearances of Christian zeal and service without having a vibrant heart that is fully alive with the Lord.

I remember a story that Mike Bickle once told. He was talking about how he had to make a hard decision regarding ministry. He was in his mid-30s, leading a church in Kansas City, Missouri, with a congregation of more than 3,000 people. He was invited by a world-renowned Christian leader, John Wimber, to speak at conferences all around the world. For three years he traveled to some very large gatherings, with over 5,000 people in attendance, speaking and ministering next to John Wimber. The following is the story shared by Mike Bickle:

> So I (Mike Bickle) went with him and all these conferences and this fanfare was happening. I was there and I did this for about three years. Lots of doors were opening and lots of new relationships were being established. Just a whole lot of buzz was going on around the things that we were doing. The Holy Spirit spoke to me and said, "I want you to tell him, 'No.'" I said, "Okay."

So I met with him (John Wimber). I said, "John, I can't travel anymore." I sat in the van and said, "I can't do any more conferences." He said, "Well, I have you signed up. You are already on five or six brochures." I said, "I will go and keep my word, but I would like you to free me. If you do not free me I will keep my word, but I won't take any more conferences." He said, "Sure, I will free you, but what is the problem?" I said, "I am backslidden!" He thought I meant I was in some scandalous sin or something like that. He said, "What!" I said, "No, no, not that way, I mean I am backslidden. When I pray and read the Word I don't weep anymore. For several years, for most days when I quieted my heart I would feel His presence. I have not wept in prayer in a year."

He said, "Okay, is that it?" I said, "That's backslidden to me, I will not live this way all of my days, I will not do this!" He said, "I appreciate that, I free you." He freed me and I went back home.[1]

This is so hard to do, but Mike saw the state of his heart and evaluated what was most important. No one publicly would have known that his heart was far away from God. No one would have noticed that his heart was not moved by God's presence.

SUBTLE DECLINE OF GREATS

Great men and women can start off with immense zeal and fervor in the Lord, hungry and desperate after God's presence and to do His exploits. However, over time their hearts can lose fervency and that holy discontentment that propels them to their knees, making them willing to do anything for love. There are various reasons why people lose their focus and do not attend to their heart or original passion. It could be the distraction of being busy, looking at accomplishments, or even comparing ministry or business size to others, all the while losing their heart's passion with the Lord. The Bible is full of examples like this.

Hezekiah was a man who started out doing some great and awesome things in the sight of the Lord.

> Hezekiah ruled in Judah 125 years after Joash. He was the son of Ahaz. Ahaz had been a very wicked king who had encouraged moral decline in Judah and had been rebellious toward the Lord. He offered sacrifices to the gods of the nations that had defeated him in battle, and he discontinued the worship of the Lord in the temple. He actually shut the doors of the temple so that no one could enter. He brought the Holy articles to the false gods in every town in Judah. And provoked the Lord to anger. Because of him, the Lord allowed Judah to be conquered by Syria (2 Chr. 28:5).[2]

In the beginning of his reign when Hezekiah became king, he turned to the Lord. He realized the poverty of the nation, which in many ways was due to their abandonment of the Lord and their worship of false gods.

> So he set out to reform the kingdom. As soon as he took the throne, he reopened the temple and had the priests work to restore everything that had been destroyed. He again employed the Levites in offering the daily sacrifices and in practicing night and day worship, according to the order of David. He called the entire nation of Israel, from the northern and southern kingdoms of Israel and Judah, to come and celebrate the Passover feast. The people returned to the Lord under his leadership, and Judah prospered greatly. The nation had not experienced the blessing of the Lord in this manner since the days of Solomon.[3]

Hezekiah began his reign with a great turning back to the Lord. He lifted his face and heart toward God, and as a leader he led his nation to do the same. Because of this, God blessed him and prospered Him.

At one point, toward the end of his life, Hezekiah became physically sick. He only had days to live. During this desperate time, Hezekiah prayed to God.

> *Then he turned his face toward the wall, and prayed to the Lord, saying, "Remember now, O Lord, I pray, how I have walked before you in truth and with a loyal heart, and have done what was good in Your sight." And Hezekiah wept bitterly* (2 Kings 20:2-3).

God heard Hezekiah's prayer, saw his heart, and responded by healing his body and granting him 15 more years of life. But over time, his heart became dull and prideful.

An example of his pride occurred during a visit from the Babylonian king, Berodach-Baladan, in Second Kings 20. Hezekiah showed the king all of his treasures of silver, gold, and trophies from wars and conquests. He presented the Babylonian king his dominion with great arrogance and pride. In essence, he was bragging about all his accolades to Israel's future enemies.

God was not pleased with Hezekiah's heart. So God sent Isaiah, the prophet, to tell him a judgment that would take place after his lifetime. Isaiah declared:

> *Hear the word of the Lord; "Behold, the days are coming when all that is in your house, and what your fathers have accumulated until this day, shall be carried to Babylon; nothing shall be left," says the Lord. "And they shall take away some of your sons who will descend from you, whom you will beget, and they shall be eunuchs in the palace of the king of Babylon"* (2 Kings 20:16-18).

Hezekiah knew from previous experience that it took humility and a surrender of his will to repent and turn to the Lord, yet at this point in his life, his heart was dull and cold. His heart was in contentment. He was in "coast mode." We know this to be the case because this is how Hezekiah responded to such a harsh judgment:

> So Hezekiah said to Isaiah, "The word of the Lord which you have spoken is good!" For he said, "Will there not be peace and truth at least in my days?" (2 Kings 20:19)

"At least in my days"! This is a shocking response. Earlier when Hezekiah was physically ill, he turned to God with his whole heart. However, when the judgment would not affect him personally, he remained complacent and comfortable, choosing to remain in his laziness instead of fighting for future generations. What a heart-wrenching state of being! He had great selfishness. He was without the foresight of what his children would have to deal with because of his own foolishness if he did not repent! All I can say is, "God save me from ever responding like this!"

THIS IS SO COMMON

We may look at the story of Hezekiah and think, *How could that happen? How could he respond like that?* Sadly this is not a rare response. The Bible is full of many more examples of this nature. I feel the need to give a few more examples of others who became dull. Some turned to God, others simply died in complacency, while others turned away from God all together.

Gideon: Even after gaining victory and popularity in the famous battle that he won with only 300 men, Gideon, his family, and all Israel turned their backs on God and worshiped a golden ephod (see Judges 7-8).

Eli: Eli was a priest of the Lord who raised the man of God, Samuel, but neglected his own house. His two sons were wicked and God rejected his entire house from being priests and ministering before Him any longer (see 1 Samuel 2-4).

Jehoshaphat: Jehoshaphat placed men at the front of his army to sing praises to the Lord. The Lord then fought for them and came against their enemies. But later the king made an alliance with Ahaziah, the wicked king from Israel (see 2 Chronicles 20).

The hardest thing to be faced with is our own barrenness. When we silence everything around us and it is just us and the Lord, we must face where we are in our heart. To be aware that we once had a passionate pursuit after God, but now do not have a pursuit at all, is a tough place to be, and one that takes great courage to admit. It spurs me on to live a life that starts well and ends even better. It is absolutely crucial that we continue to go after God all the days of our lives. These and other examples laced throughout Scripture are there to show us that no matter how "on fire" we were yesterday, it is so easy to fall away, grow cold, and have a dull heart.

Many are living off what they once had and once knew. They are running on fumes from yesterday and stale bread from six months or even five years ago.

Now if you are being stirred and wondering how you can tell if there is any dullness or disconnection with the God who is living inside you, I want to show you a really easy way to examine your heart—through your speech.

A REFLECTION OF THE HEART

Words are a reflection of the heart. We can evaluate the quality of our heart by examining our speech. If our words are dark, negative, or sinful, what does that tell us about our heart?

For out of the abundance of the heart the mouth speaks (Matthew 12:34).

The abundance of the heart is the overflow. We only get out of our heart what has been put into it. For example, a glass will be filled with whatever you put into it. You cannot draw sewage from a glass of pure water, and you cannot draw pure water from a glass of sewage. What we value internally comes out externally through our words. Jesus called this the "good treasure" or the "evil treasure." What we value most cannot remain hidden; it will be revealed in our speech.[4]

A good man out of the good treasure of his heart brings forth good things; and an evil man out of the evil treasure brings forth evil things (Matthew 12:35).

Our words show us the direction we are pointing. If our words are wholesome, we are pointed toward what is good; if our words are defiled and corrupt, we are pointed toward evil. I can measure and evaluate so much of the abundance of my heart by what I say and the manner in which it comes out.

Just recently, the Holy Spirit spoke to me about the harshness of how I spoke to some of my staff. He wasn't highlighting the content of what I said, but the manner in which I said it. There was harshness in my tone that revealed bitterness in my heart. He showed me three instances in one week, two of the times were one on one and the other time was when I was publicly teaching. He showed me the rough overtones that came out, that really didn't have anything to do with the people, but revealed the state of my heart. What I spend time doing and what I think about, eventually will come out through my speech, and it did. I was so thankful for God revealing my heart to me by showing me the words and tone of my words and "the well" from which they came.

Breaking through Dullness

Draw me after you and let us run together! (Song of Solomon 1:4 NASB)

My good friend Corey Stark shared a dream he once had that I feel is important to share with you:

> I had a dream that I was driving a car. In the dream I got out of the car and I noticed that the tank was leaking gas. In the dream I understood that God was communicating to me that my ministry and my life, which was the car, had things in it that were letting the fuel out of my walk with God; out of my spiritual life. Things that were depleting my fuel. The application of this dream was that the Lord was wanting me to eliminate things that were distracting me, causing me to lose the very thing that I was trying to put into my life—intimacy with God. I really had to take a hard look at the things that were distracting my eyes, my ears and really depleting my energy or my fuel in intimacy with Him.[5]

Answer to the State of Our Heart

I want to devote the rest of this chapter to what I believe are the answers for reviving a dull heart. If your heart has found itself in a state of dullness, sleepiness, lack of desperation or hunger for God and His ways, I want to show you some answers for turning on the light and reviving your heart to start beating again. You weren't meant to live in a status quo love, but instead, a life passionately pursuing the One you love. Let's begin with what I believe to be the first step.

RETURNING TO OUR FIRST LOVE

In the book of Revelation, Jesus is speaking to the seven churches, giving some of them warning signs and some praises. With His warning signs, He gives direction for what the church needs to do to change. I want to turn your attention to the church of Ephesus.

> *To the angel of the church of Ephesus write...I know your works, your labor, your patience, and that you cannot bear those who are evil. And you have tested those who say they are apostles and are not, and have found them liars; and you have persevered and have patience, and have labored for My name's sake and have not become weary. Nevertheless I have this against you, that you have left your first love. Remember therefore from where you have fallen; repent and do the first works, or else I will come to you quickly and remove your lampstand from its place—unless you repent* (Revelation 2:1-5).

The Ephesian church is an extraordinary church. They are exceptional, and this is the church most people would love to be part of. Look at some of these attributes that Jesus Himself says about them:

- They are hardworking.

- They are a persevering church with great patience.

- They remained steady and faithful under pressure for many years.

- They labored for God's name sake and didn't become weary. In other words they were zealous to establish a true biblical message and to maintain diligent outreach to others.

- The Ephesians could not bear those who were evil; they would not tolerate false ministries who promoted impurity (doctrinally and morally).

- They *"tested those who say they are apostles and are not, and have found them liars."* They "tested" the visiting ministries and required that they hold to biblical standards.

Regardless, Jesus has something against this church, saying, *"Nevertheless I have this against you, that you have left your first love"* (Rev 2:4). This is quite an indictment. Mike Bickle suggests, "They put labor and growing their ministry reaching into all Asia, before cultivating a heart of love for Jesus. The first and great commandment is to love God with all our heart. This will empower us to love people much deeper and with consistency. Lovers always outwork workers. They became like the foolish virgins in the parable in Mt. 25:1-13."[6]

The Ephesian church left their first love—they neglected their original heart of devotion for Jesus that was seen in the great revival in which the church was started in Acts 19. Service and doctrinal purity are very important, but they can never replace our love for Jesus.

EXHORTATION TO RESPOND: REMEMBER, REPENT, ACT

Remember therefore from where you have fallen; repent and do the first works, or else I will come to you quickly and remove your lampstand from its place—unless you repent (Revelation 2:5).

Notice in Revelation 2:5 with Mike Bickle that "Jesus gave this church a three-step process to restore their love: remember, repent, and act.

Remember from where you have fallen—they were to remember how they used to feel about Jesus. We are to think on God's past goodness to us and our past love and devotion for Jesus. They left their love for Jesus, but not their hatred for evil.

Repent and do the first works—they were to repent of their negligence and then act in ways that would fan the flame of their affection for Him. To repent is to "change our mind and life vision" to agree with devotion for Jesus. The first works are those first in priority to God, and those that we originally embraced in our walk with Jesus. Loving is top priority to God.

I will remove your lampstand from its place—the lampstand of a ministry speaks of their witness to others in the nations. A lamp often speaks of one's ministry as it brings God's light to others (Mt. 5:15-16). Ephesus was the bright light of all Asia. The ministry that loses its tender love of Jesus will soon lose its light of ministry even if it is diligent in service and sound in doctrine.[7]

To summarize, we must consciously cultivate the ability to be responsive to God with wholehearted love. The Lord speaks of our first love as a height—a glorious, wonderful height. We forsake—not lose—our first love, meaning that we leave that place of spiritual passion by the choices we make and the lifestyles we adopt. Our first love is not something we accidentally misplace, but run away from. Believers who have left their first love must return and do their *"first works."* Service without the foundation of intimacy with Jesus leads to burn out, disappointment, and wounding.

DO YOU REMEMBER?

My friend Corey Russell has several anointed preaching and praying CDs with prophetic music that I listen to all the time. One in particular, called *Ancient Paths,* is very powerful and has helped shape some of my thinking. I will share with you what I sense the Holy Spirit wants to infuse in us as He calls us back to His heart.

I believe that God is speaking to His people again. He's wooing them, alluring them, and saying: *I want you to know My heart, I want you to know the heartbeat of it all.*

I believe God is fighting for the hearts of His people, calling us back to the place where we went after Him. He says, "I remember how you used to love Me. I remember how you used to go after Me. Like Mary of Bethany, how she poured her love onto the feet of Jesus; she didn't count the cost. This whole thing is about love. Do you remember when you said *"yes"*? I want it like it was in the old days when you went after Me in the wilderness."

I believe God is telling us how much He misses us. He misses you. He wants a newness of the love you once had. Do you remember those early days of salvation when all you had to hear was the name Jesus and you wept? You used to yearn just to be with Jesus. Jesus wasn't just part of your life, He was the very essence of your life. You had to know the kiss of His Word. The Word was alive to your heart as you encountered Him. He was your very heart breathing. You had to be with Him.

> God is crying out to us: "You fell out of love!" Do you hear His cry? He is crying, with overwhelming emotion, saying: "Return! When did you fall out of love with me? Return to me. Return." It's about yearning again. It's about longing and a reaching. It is about a missing and going after Him, in your heart. If we settle for anything less we lost it all. It's about that simple adoration. What happened to the purity of devotion? You were in love.[8]

KEEP THE FIRE BURNING

To close this chapter, I want to let you in on one of the questions I have asked many friends and leaders in hopes to take hold of something that would encourage, inspire, or challenge me in my pursuit of keeping my heart alive. The main reason I wrote this chapter: keeping my heart alive is one of the main issues of my life over which I have to keep diligent and watchful. This is one of the central themes that both Christelle and I are watching in our lives and in the lives of our children.

One thing is for sure, it's not necessarily how you start this journey with God, but how you finish that matters. I don't see anything else that I desire other than to aim at having a heart fully alive in God. I know that everything else flows from this. The question of how to keep my heart alive is ever before me.

The following application comes from a discussion I had with friends about this very issue. I pray this will encourage and challenge you at the same time!

> *And the fire on the altar shall be kept burning on it; it shall not be put out. And the priest shall burn wood on it every morning, and lay the burnt offering in order on it; and he shall burn on it the fat of the peace offerings. A fire shall always be burning on the altar; it shall never go out* (Leviticus 6:12-13).

God commanded that the fire on the altar should never go out. This description represents the fire or presence of God on our hearts. God repeated this command in this portion of Scripture. Let's break down the three aspects of keeping the fire burning found in this Scripture and what they represent:

- The altar represents our hearts.
- The fire represents the presence of God.

- The wood represents the positive things that we put in to keep that fire or intimacy with God alive.

What's important to understand first is that the fire was God's responsibility. The fire upon the altar came from heaven. He provides the divine fire. He starts the fire in our hearts. However, it's our job to sustain the fire and not let the fire go out. He commands this fire never to go out.

It's our privilege to get the wood, which represents doing the natural, positive things to maintain a fire in our hearts.

There were three types of fire, or piles of wood, found in this portion of Scripture, for maintaining the fire continually; some were large, on which the daily sacrifice was burnt; the second had less, and they called this the pile of incense, because they took from it fire in a censer to burn the morning and evening incense; and the third was only for preserving the fire that it might not go out at night.

These three piles of wood are a prophetic picture of the three basic things we are to do in gathering wood for the fire on our hearts. Here they are:

- A life of prayer.
- A life in the Word of God.
- A life in fellowship with the Holy Spirit.

These three woodpiles represent what is needed for sustaining a heart that is alive or burning for God from the inside out. This is living a life in constant communion with God.

This should also be a daylong focus, where you're speaking to the Holy Spirit about the Word. You're looking to encounter the Man-Jesus between the lines, not just intellectual information.

Without this stoking of the fire morning and night, you will easily let the fire go out. It's too easy for one day to become two and before you know it, five days becomes one month. One month can easily turn to one, two, or three years. It's a slow process that eventually lets the fire of God's presence go out. I tell you this by personal experience. Once again I urge you, don't let the fire go out; kindle it today!

I encourage you with everything in me to take this advice seriously, to take the steps to "get wood" and sustain the fire in your heart. Don't just have a faint little light glimmering, but have the indwelling, filling, empowering, illuminating, nourishing presence of the Holy Spirit of God, *burning deeply* in your heart. This fire should be *intense, fervent*, and *never ceasing*!

If you don't have fire in your heart, or if it has become faint, then start gathering the wood. If you have let the fire go out, turn to God now, begin speaking with Him and make a plan to get wood daily through living a life of the Word, a life of prayer, and a life in fellowship with the Holy Spirit. There's no better way to live!

APOSTOLIC MANDATE: PRAYER AND THE WORD

Let me end this chapter by demonstrating this point with one other example. Let's look at the apostles in the book of Acts. How did they live?

But we will give ourselves continually to prayer and to the ministry of the word (Acts 6:4).

The first apostolic mandate was to live sustained lives in prayer and the Word. In Acts 6:4 we see that the apostles devoted themselves to continually live a life of prayer and to the ministry of the Word. This enabled and empowered them to do great exploits, not the other way around.

There is evidence that the apostles practiced this lifestyle of prayer and ministry of the Word in Acts 2 and Acts 4. Jesus' instructions before He left were to wait in prayer until they were endued with power from on high. The way the apostles lived serves as an example of how we are to live, lead, and minister. In fact, if we are not endued with power from on high, there really is little or no point except to get a badge to say that we served, but with very little results, if any. I know this may sound harsh, but primacy of prayer over and above preaching or any capacity of serving is the key to protecting ourselves from a dull heart.

Leonard Ravenhill, who confronts the lack of spiritual alertness in his book *Why Revival Tarries,* says, "No man is greater than his prayer life."[9] The importance of talking to God about men before talking to men about God is first and foremost how we should live. I say again, this is not optional but the only way to live to sustain a heart fully alive.

Let me ask you, what is the ratio of prayer to ministry in our daily lives? From a contemporary mindset we might assume that the majority of time spent by the apostles was "doing" ministry (that being the "most important" thing). Yet the testimony of Luke in the book of Acts seems to indicate the primacy of prayer and communion with the Lord above ministry of the Word. This is the most important thing!

I started this chapter with Proverbs 4:23, *"Keep your heart with all diligence, for out of it spring the issues of life."* This is a proverb from Solomon that I consider of utmost importance. So keep your heart alive, and be watchful to that end, for everything else in your life flows from this!

Chapter 10

STRONG IN SPIRIT

But those whose hope is in the Lord
shall renew their strength.

—ISAIAH

Have you ever wondered how to get spiritual strength? We were meant to be strong in spirit; and in order to be strong in spirit, we must walk by the Spirit of God.

An example of physical strength we see in the Bible is Samson. Where did Samson get his great strength? Have you ever wondered about that? In Sunday school all of the pictures portray Samson as some kind of superhuman, physical specimen, capable of killing and destroying the Philistines. Samson would have not had that extraordinary physical strength apart from God giving it to him. He was given an anointing or a gift of supernatural strength. But nowhere in the Bible does it indicate that Samson had the appearance of strength *physically*. In fact, Scriptures seem to indicate that the Philistines actually wondered where he got his strength, and I can only assume it is because he did not have the appearance of being strong, for none of the texts actually say he was strong in appearance.

Judges 16:5 says, "*The lords of the Philistines came up to her* [Delilah] *and said to her, 'entice him, and find out where his great strength lies, and by what means we may overpower him, that we may bind him to afflict him.'"* As you can tell, Samson's strength was a supernatural strength that affected the natural. If Samson was indeed strong in appearance it was never mentioned, but he was, however, physically strong when the Spirit of the Lord came upon him.

God calls every believer to walk in strength, a spiritual strength that comes from Him—*strength of spirit.* This type of strength has to be developed. In the same way you go into strict training of your body to achieve a goal in health and fitness, you also go into strict spiritual training to develop a spirit that is stronger than anything you may encounter in life that opposes God. You see, although Samson was given a gift and anointing from God, it did not strengthen him spiritually; he actually had a feeble and weak spirit. His weak spirit, which we see time and again in his life story, failed to help him resist sin, grow in God, and fulfill the destiny that his gift was given to help fulfill. Although he ended his life knowing God, he lived it unable to stand against temptation in spite of the great gift of physical strength he was given, because having a strong gifting does not equal a strong spirit.

We as believers must *strengthen ourselves in the Lord* (see 1 Sam. 30:6). I am not talking about strength that we have to make up or becoming some sort of optimist. I am talking about relying on God and building our spirit on a steady diet of the things of God.

> *Everyone who competes in the games goes into strict training* (1 Corinthians 9:25 NIV).

We need to put our spirit into training to the point that it strengthens every aspect of our lives, the lives of those around us, and those we touch. I am talking about a strength that affects the natural realm because of our inner strength, walking in step with and full of the Holy Spirit, and having a spirit self that is built up and ready for anything.

STRONG OR WEAK

Be strong in the Lord and the power of His might (Ephesians 6:10).

If we are not strong, we are weak. There is no passive existence in between, where we just stand still. If we are not moving forward, we are moving backward. As we grow in strength by setting our minds and actions to do it, we become stronger each day. But it is a choice that only we can make. When we do our part and place our hearts before God, committed to doing what is necessary to grow, He does His part and we grow strong. Why would you want to live your life in a place of weakness anyway? Being spiritually lazy, by neglecting to do what it takes to grow in God, is something we cannot afford. Many Christians today live wimpy and wilted, like a willow tree. They take no clear stance and walk in more fear of man than fear of God. There is so much confusion and passivity. This thinking even presents itself as caution and intelligence, but really it is dressed-up unbelief and compromise. God is raising up men and women who are mighty in word and deed because their spirits are strong. Our enemy the devil is prowling, looking to pounce on and attack the weak.

GROWING IN SPIRIT

And the Child grew and became strong in spirit, filled with wisdom; and the grace of God was upon Him (Luke 2:40).

The Bible says that both Jesus and John the Baptist grew in spirit and in wisdom and stature. Even as a child, Jesus grew and became progressively mighty in His spirit. He became strong in His spirit. This is what God wants to awaken in our hearts. Now, in our mind we could dismiss Jesus as growing in spirit simply because He is God, but I want to point out He is also a man who walked the earth like you and I. And how about John the Baptist, can you dismiss his growth in strength of spirit? What about the many greats in the Scriptures and throughout history whose lives show the evidence of their obvious effort to have a strong spirit?

Let's take a look at another man in Scripture, Joseph. Most know his story, but let's briefly look at it again. After declaring the dreams that he had to his brothers, they sold him, which resulted in him losing his family and being a slave. He was sold to a merchant named Potiphar, an officer of Pharaoh, where in spite of all of his major struggles, Joseph remained steady in his resolve to honor God; the Lord blessed him and favored him.

> *The Lord was with Joseph, and he was a successful man; and he was in the house of his master the Egyptian. And his master saw that the Lord was with him and that the Lord made all he did to prosper in his hand* (Genesis 39:2-3).

God was with Joseph; what an amazing reality. God *"made all he did to prosper in his hand."* Joseph loved God and demonstrated it through his obedience and fear of God.

> *So it was, as she spoke to Joseph day by day, that he did not heed her, to lie with her or to be with her. But it happened about this time, when Joseph went into the house to do his work, and none of the men of the house was inside, that she caught him by his garment, saying, "Lie with me." But he left his garment in her hand, and fled and ran outside* (Genesis 39:10-12).

When confronted day by day, being pressed and tempted by Potiphar's wife to sleep with her, Joseph aggressively refused. Even when she took hold of his clothes, he ran. He had a resolve in his heart that he would honor God, even when confronted with the greatest moral assault of his life. This is a great example of a man whose spirit is stronger than his body and mind. And Joseph could have probably gotten away with sleeping with her, since Potiphar *"left all that he had in Joseph's hand, and did not know what he had except for the bread which he ate"* (Gen. 39:6). But Joseph knew that God saw him; he had an honor, love, awe, and loyalty to his God that rose up within him and helped him in the time of temptation.

He had invested in his spirit and trained it to the point that it was ready to resist sin in the hour of testing, when it was right before him. I love that Joseph had enough strength to not only resist sin, but he literally ran away from it and removed himself with great exertion from the situation. I also love that Joseph could have been angry at God for giving him the dream, allowing him to be sold into slavery, spending so much time in prison, being falsely accused, and receiving years of unjust treatment, but he did not blame God. Joseph was faithful to God and even to the covenant of his family.

Joseph was determined to love God, honor those around him, and say no to sin. And he was not only resolved, he was ready. When we really look at the difficulties of Joseph's life, most of us would have given up, but he did not. How could he do this? The answer is simple—Joseph was strong in spirit. His spirit was strong in the Lord. Joseph had something built up in him that was able to lead his physical body. The physical body has no conscience; all it knows is desire and seeking its own pleasure. Your conscience, however, is made up of your spirit and your soul; it understands covenants, laws, commitments, and morality. Joseph had developed his spirit to be able to lead his body.

He was a man of character, with his focus on God. Joseph didn't rely on his position of authority, physical strength, wealth, prophetic dreams, or anointing. He had built up such a history with God that the strength in which he built his spirit not only saved him, but also saved his people and nation.

A spiritually weak person has a weak spirit; and frankly most Christians do nothing about it. The majority of believers live their lives being led by their body and even their soul with all of its appetites. When we choose to do nothing to strengthen our spirit, we live a pathetic, passive existence, just barely living at all, coasting on our anointing and gifting alone or past experiences. It is certain that the fruit of this kind of life is as it is written, problems and difficulties refer to fruit, not life problems and difficulties—results of a spirit that is not only weak but is in the intensive care unit of the hospital.

Now, going back to Samson we see that he is the perfect example of this. Samson started out being supernaturally empowered by God with great anointing. He had supernatural strength not because of who he was or anything he did. If you read the account of Samson's life, God blessed Samson with power because of his parents and the desperate need the nation of Israel found herself in (see Judges 13).

Many problems started when Samson decided to walk in rebellion and do things his way. One of the ways he compromised was when he wanted to marry someone outside of his tribe. He looked for a wife in a people who did not honor God and worshiped other dead gods. He had no moral absolutes; he was following his own ideas, his physical desires, and a lifestyle of dishonor to God. And as I stated earlier, Samson failed to recognize that although he had great physical strength, it obviously did not mean he had strength spiritually. He did not honor the gifts he was given, his parents, his God, or his prophetic history. God set this man apart from birth and he didn't seem to care. Samson lived in such a way that his body or carnal desires governed his life. This is what led Samson's life. He married and slept with women who were not faithful to him or his God. Samson was a weak man, even though he had a great anointing in his life.

ANOINTING VERSUS STRONG IN SPIRIT

There is a massive difference between having a strong anointing of God and being strong in spirit in your inner being. Samson was strong in anointing, which for him was his physical strength. There are many other examples of men and women who are anointed to do great things, but have very little strength in spirit to combat sin and go forward pursuing God.

Christian history is full of men who were anointed by God but failed to keep their spirit strong. I have personally been with many Christian leaders who walked in great anointing in public, but behind the scenes, when the anointing was gone, lived their lives in compromise and casualness toward sin and God's ways of living. I am saying this to warn of the danger of ignoring our need to grow in strength of spirit and having a weak inner self. How we live before a meeting, during the meeting, and after the meeting, so to speak, is of utmost importance. God is more concerned with the strength of our spirit before the meeting and after the meeting than what a person has been anointed to do.

You may not be on a stage, but this principle applies to all. God has given us giftings and anointing to walk out in life to fulfill His purposes on the earth in partnership with us. No matter what you are called to do for and with God, you are first called to have a strong spirit and a life of vibrancy inside, to be alive in God, living with great character in your inner and outer life. The gifts God gives each of us are great gifts, but I am merely pointing out that this is not to be confused with having the strength to live a life in God. Being strong in spirit, having an unwavering resolve to live righteously and walking it out in your choices, is not a gift from God but comes through a daily discipline of a life submitted to God. Building a strong spirit takes time, diligence, and training, and only we can make the decision to take on and do this training.

Anointing does not help us when we are confronted with temptations or life's pressures; a strong spirit does. You must have something built up in you. The difference between Samson and Joseph was the strength on the inside. Samson had a great anointing, but was weak in spirit. Joseph was favored by God, had great character and a strong spirit. If we don't build a strong spirit, we may be able to operate or facilitate God's anointing, but could still have disastrous lives. We can have strong anointings but lose our ability to discern temptation, wrong situations, wrong thoughts, wrong emotions, and wrong relationships.

Anointings are for moments but do not guarantee success—having a strong spirit does. Your strength is not measured by your anointing. Your strength is based on how you live your life daily, especially behind closed doors, when no one else sees. You can't measure maturity in a person's life by the gifts of the Spirit they operate in, such as prophecy, healing, deliverance, or the gift of faith. But you *can* measure their life by how much fruit of the Spirit they have, such as love, joy, peace, patience, and self-control (see Gal. 5:22-23). We often measure spiritual maturity by the gifts of the Spirit that a person walks in, but those are only gifts and do not indicate maturity. The fruit of the Spirit is what we must determine to have and to walk in. Gifting doesn't equal character, and anointing doesn't equal maturity (see 1 Cor. 12). Just because someone is gifted doesn't mean that God is endorsing every area of his or her life or his or her ministry style. Character is much more important to the Lord than gifting.

> *No good tree bears bad fruit, nor does a bad tree bear good fruit. Each tree is recognized by its own fruit* (Luke 6:43-44 NIV).

> *But the fruit of the Spirit is love, joy, peace, patience, kindness, goodness, faithfulness, gentleness and self-control. Against such things there is no law* (Galatians 5:22-23 NIV).

I have also met and known great men and women who not only pursued the gifts, but also had great fruit of the Spirit in their lives. They didn't rely on anointing but desired strength of spirit. These people are not perfect, but they pursue and are focused on God and building an interior life that leads their soul and physical body.

BUILDING A STRONG SPIRIT

Okay, so how do you build a strong spirit? How do you set your life on course to walk like Joseph and so many other great men and women of God? There is no other way to say it than to take the greatest invitation to commune with God. He is our sustenance; God invites us to taste of Him, to look at Him, to walk with Him, to breathe of His life, to know Him. This is what creates strength and sustains us.

I am going to share with you, not so much of things to do, but ways to eat, drink, and commune.

HIDING THE WORD IN YOUR HEART

Your word I have hidden in my heart, that I might not sin against You (Psalm 119:11).

To really begin to have a strong spirit man, we must hide God's Word in our heart. God writes His Word on our heart as we live by it. I can't say this enough—we are to live spiritually healthy in our heart by feeding on God's Word, which is the holy transcript of His heart. Our heart lives and becomes strong and healthy by feeding on God's Word in spirit and truth. The opposite is also true. Our heart dies and becomes weak and sick without feeding on God's Word. The most substantial way in which we feed our spirit and bolster our spiritual strength is by feeding on God's Word in spirit and truth.

PRAYER LIFE

Prayer. What is prayer? Let's begin there. Prayer is communication between you and God. Prayer is the words and affections interchanged between God and humans, the Creator and the created. God desires communion, and the way to make that possible is through prayer. It is fellowship and communion with God. Prayer is access to God at the highest form.

Richard J. Foster, in his book *Prayer,* says, "We are attracted to it and repelled by it. We believe prayer is something we should do, even something we want to do, but it seems like a chasm stands between us and actually praying. We experience the agony of prayerlessness."[1]

I know this all too well. It's such a tragedy that Christians can live their entire Christian existence without the reality of a life of prayer, communion, and intimacy with God. "A prayer-less life is of the chief disasters in a Christian life. A lack of prayer closes heaven and closes your heart to Him. If we are unwilling to change, we will abandon prayer as a noticeable characteristic of our lives. The closer we come to the heartbeat of God the more we see our need and the more we desire to be conformed to Christ."[2]

In his classic book on prayer, E.M. Bounds writes, "Failure to pray is a failure along the whole line of life. It is a failure of duty, service, and spiritual progress. God must help man in prayer. He who does not pray, therefore robs himself of God's help and places God where He cannot help man. Man must pray to God if love for God is going to exist."[3]

Prayer is more than just spitting out words in the air. Prayer more than just reaches heaven—our prayers reach the heart of God. Prayer expresses our heart. Prayer changes our heart. The powerful part about prayer is that our prayers have the power to change cities, shift atmospheres, move angels and demons; it is the way the government of God works. And sustained prayer releases God's justice on the earth (making wrong things right). Isn't this incredible?

Prayer does so much; I could go on and on. I haven't even scratched the surface of the power and benefit of prayer. There are all kinds of prayers and many forms. There is the prayer of petition, prayer of thanksgiving, prayer of agreement, prayer of faith, prayer of intercession, and others. But I am forever marked by one powerful truth about prayer. My prayers touch God's heart, and when He speaks, His words touch my heart. That's enough for me. Your words, overflowing from your heart, touch God. This is the greatest privilege and reality there is.

Jesus knew this reality while He lived on this earth. God Himself prayed to the Father. He separated Himself regularly and Scripture makes sure that we know the secret to His strength. Jesus obviously walked this way for the disciples to ask Him to teach them how to pray. Let me show you the commentary that was given of Jesus' life in the book of Mark. *"Now in the morning, having risen a long while before daylight, He went out and departed to a solitary place; and there He prayed"* (Mark 1:35). He lived a life of prayer and He lives a life of prayer still. He lives to make intercession for us (see Heb. 7:24-25). If Jesus walked this way on earth and walks this way still, do we see the power of the God-Man Jesus doing this even now?

A life of prayer is a choice—but really a life of prayer is a must. This is a life of strength, living in communion and living connected to the Life Source through prayer.

PRAY-READING THE WORD

To bring together these two lifestyles of hiding God's Word in your heart and living a life of prayer, let me launch you into one of the greatest tools of communion with God. We have an invitation from Jesus Himself to eat of Him, to dine with Him, to drink of Him. Psalm 23 is a picture of that invitation. He prepares a table before us and invites us to eat with Him and of Him. He is Himself the host and the food. He leads us beside still waters, He invites us to walk with Him, talk with Him; He gives us rest, and He restores our soul. That means He brings to life those things inside of us that were dead as a result of stress, anxiety, and fears. He renews, brings sustenance, and brings nourishment. This all sounds wonderful, but how? Let's look at the life-giving Word in this well-known passage of Psalm 23 and use it to practically apply to our life.

> *The Lord is my shepherd; I shall not want. He makes me to lie down in green pastures; He leads me beside the still waters. He restores my soul; He leads me in the paths of righteousness for His name's sake. Yea, though I walk through the valley of the shadow of death, I will fear no evil; for You are with me; Your rod and Your staff, they comfort me. You prepare a table before me in the presence of my enemies; You anoint my head with oil; my cup runs over. Surely goodness and mercy shall follow me all the days of my life; and I will dwell in the house of the Lord forever* (Psalm 23:1-6).

Something remarkable happens when we eat of Him and drink of Him. We become strengthened and energized. We experience *"rivers of living water"* flowing in us, through us, and out of us (see John 7:38).

How do we walk this out daily in our lives? First we must begin by quieting our mind. We must be still before God. We must calm ourselves and quiet ourselves by laying aside all of the day's concerns. We invite the Holy Spirit to come, and then we begin. Take one line of Psalm 23 for example and say it out loud, slowly, and deliberately. Slow your mind...way down. Approach the Lord in quietness. Quiet your intensity; quiet everything that normally races through your mind and just say the words: "The Lord is my Shepherd." Then let Him talk to you by saying what He wants you to know through that powerful statement: I am your Shepherd. You are my sheep. You have no needs. I take care of you. I have given you rest. I am rest. I am your food. I am all you need and more. I am the only real food there is. I am restoring your soul. I am giving you real water. I am water that satisfies your thirst. I am your leader. I am with you. You are in me and I in you. I am goodness that follows you all your days. I have always been there. I will always be there. I am all that is good. I am beside you. I am in you.

Doing this is called pray-reading the Word. But it is really so much more than that, it is talking to God and letting Him talk to you. The Word is alive. Let this Word be life to your physical body and your spirit. Talk slowly to God and let Him talk through you, to you. It is life-changing and simple to talk to God and have Him talk right back to you.

In Psalm 23 God was talking to David, revealing Himself to David; but more than that, He was revealing Himself to us. He is the same God as the God of David. He placed the longing to know Him within us so that we will seek Him; He has the same longing for us as we do for Him. He wants to be known by you. If you talk to God this way and let Him talk to you this way, you won't find your mind wandering or watching the clock to see when devotions are over. You will experience the rivers of living water as they flow from your innermost being. You will feel what it means to be alive, and you will know God like you never have before.

This practice of quieting ourselves, being still and reading the Bible and talking to God, will awaken in you a life of the Word and a life of the Spirit. Once you have tasted this, you will never again want to only read the Bible without talking to God, or pray prayers based solely out of emotion. You will encounter the living Word between the lines and you will experience the tangible presence of His Spirit.

FASTING

I was led into a state of great dissatisfaction with my own want of stability in faith and love…I often felt myself weak in the presence of temptation and needed frequently to hold days of fasting and prayer...that would enable me efficiently to labor. —Charles G. Finney [4]

Fasting is sometimes an unknown or scary subject for those who have never tried it. Fasting reminds us that our spirit, soul, and body are connected and cannot be separated. Humans are physical beings forever. We are not trying to escape our bodies. As Christians we look forward to the day when our bodies will be resurrected in glory.

Fasting quickens our spiritual appetites, sharpens our spiritual discernment, combats our trust in our own strength, and weakens the cravings of our flesh. Over-eating and overindulging causes the spirit to grow dim and dull. Spiritual sharpness is diminished, and spiritual discernment wanes.

Fasting tenderizes our hearts, softens us to the ways of God, and sharpens our discernment. In fasting, we refuse to satisfy our physical bodies and our souls with our usual comforts that actually drain our strength and hinder us from moving forward in the grace of God. Fasting is the great detoxification of our soul. As we give ourselves to fasting, God increases true spiritual hunger and expands our capacity for intimacy, revelation, and spiritual discernment.

In fasting we embrace voluntary weakness in order to embrace God's strength as our solution. Increasing our spiritual clout before others is not the purpose of fasting. In fasting, we place ourselves weak before God asking for a breakthrough in His strength.

His strength becomes our true hope and ultimate solution to our problems.

BUILDING YOURSELF UP

But you, beloved, building yourselves up on your most holy faith, praying in the Holy Spirit (Jude 20).

The apostle Jude is exhorting us to build ourselves up by praying in the Spirit, praying in tongues. This is an invitation and an encouragement to do this ourselves. God doesn't do this for us, but we do this ourselves and the way we build ourselves up is by praying in tongues.

You see, when we pray in tongues we edify ourselves. When we pray in tongues we are not strengthening others but ourselves, our interior life. That is why Paul said in First Corinthians 14:4 that, *"He who speaks in a tongue edifies himself"* or in other words, building ourselves in our inner being.

I couldn't agree more with my friend Corey Russell who wrote a powerful book called *The Glory Within* when he said, "Nothing can build me up as effectively as praying in the Holy Spirit for extended periods of time. No teaching or impartation or prophecy can replace the power of my spirit rising up and bringing my mind, will, emotions, and body into alignment with the Holy Spirit as I speak in tongues."[5]

Praying in tongues is that supercharge that boosts me spiritually like nothing else in my Christian walk. The more I partake of this divine gift, the more my spirit gets stronger and the more I want to continue in this prayer life. This is one way I get to pray in the spirit continually, and I am strengthening and edifying myself over and over and over again. I am really building a stronghold for God in my interior. And I promise you, praying in the Spirit will overflow and affect your circumstance and much more. If you would like to know more, I have written more about praying in tongues and fasting in my book *Relentless Pursuit*. I encourage you to read this and begin diving into the Word of God—you will see how this powerful gift is available to you and how it is one of the greatest weapons and tools for your life!

CONTINUAL FILLING

And do not be drunk with wine...but be filled with the Spirit, speaking to one another in psalms and hymns and spiritual songs, singing and making melody in your heart to the Lord, giving thanks always for all things to God the Father in the name of our Lord Jesus Christ (Ephesians 5:18-20).

Paul commands us *not to be drunk with wine but be filled with the Spirit.* "The Greek word for filled is *pleroo* ("play-ro-o"). It means "to fill and disperse throughout one's soul."[6] This literally is a command to *keep on presently being filled to the brim with the Spirit.* Therefore, though we receive a most definite "baptism in the Holy Spirit," we eagerly desire and pursue to be constantly filled over and over in Him. "The ongoing experience of being filled with the Spirit infuses us with everything we need to live like Jesus and bring God's will on earth as it is in heaven."[7]

This verse not only lays out what we are commanded to do in being filled with the Spirit but also invites us to pursue some very practical things to do on a daily basis in our quest to be continually filled with the Spirit of God. I urge you to take hold of these truths and fill yourself with the Spirit of God to overflowing. These are keys for our life in Him.

First, speak to one another in *psalms.* This is an invitation to speak and sing using the Psalms as well as other Scriptures of the Bible. Speaking and singing the Scriptures is so powerful. The best way to describe it to you is when you read Scripture and pray-read the Scriptures, it takes time to digest, through meditation and pondering. Singing the Scriptures is so connected to my spirit that it feels like I am drinking through a funnel (of God's truth, not needing to digest it but drinking it in quickly). Reading and meditation of the Scriptures feels like I am eating, while singing the Scriptures feels like I am drinking in God's greatness and truth.

Second, we are invited to speak to one another in *hymns and spiritual songs*. Singing hymns is the use of *previously written songs as worship to God*. Singing pre-written songs are a kick-start to connecting to God. When you start your prayer times or devotions, this is a great way to start. Many times you need something to jump-start your time with God, to get the focus off of you and onto God. Let me add to this by saying that songs that are focused on God and His majesty are the best worship songs. There are many songs that focus on "me" and what "we" are going to do for Him and how we feel. Although these songs are fine, they can take the focus off God and make it about us.

Majesty-driven songs, however, are songs that focus on God's majestic attributes; they are sung to God and are about God, these are the best songs to worship and draw us to Him. God is the solution to all of our problems. God is the answer to all of our needs; God is the very thing we long for. God is the all-merciful One, the all-consuming Fire; He's the Lifter of our head, the everlasting Love, and so much more.

God-focused or majesty-driven songs catapult us into looking at how great and beautiful God is. Singing songs with this focus strengthens and deepens our resolve to love and adore Him. He is our reward. He is absolute truth. He is absolute beauty. He is the absolute good in our lives. "We can only worship that which fascinates us."[8] "There is a mysterious fascination that carries the heart beyond itself."[9] When whole congregations join together in fascination with God by singing straight to Him, the Creator of the universe, this is when we come into agreement with the angels of heaven who worship who they see—God.

Corporate worship times should include some key ingredients. First of all worship should have admiration of God. Admiration of God esteems and marvels at who He is and what He has done. We could spend a lot of time describing God in this way, and a great corporate worship time should always begin here. *"For God is the King of all the earth; sing praises with understanding"* (Ps. 47:7).

Another key ingredient of worship is honor of God. Honor recognizes the infinity and magnitude that God holds and is. There is no one like Him; there never was and never will be. His infinite greatness is unsearchable, and our worship songs should sing of Him in this way. This places God in the rightful place in our hearts; and when a group of people unify in honor of God, we come into agreement with heaven on this alone. *"Great is the Lord, and greatly to be praised; and His greatness is unsearchable"* (Ps. 145:3).

Then it should include affectionate love toward God. This really brings honor and admiration together. Love brings great delight in God's presence and grief when we are distant. "Love when it lets itself go and no longer has any restraints, becomes adoration."[10]

When using these words to describe some key ingredients about worship, "we need to refine our definitions. Such words as honor, love and adore don't mean what they are supposed to mean. We use divine language in such a common way that when we try to rise to the exalted and divine level we find ourselves using words that do not express anything… We have spoiled them and made them common, yet they belong to God."[11]

I don't mean to downplay songs that sincerely want to build "me" up, but this is not worship of God. To worship God is the worship of a Person who is in a real place, who sits on a real throne; we are to sing straight to Him, adoring, honoring, and loving Him. When we sing songs that are not worship, we really lose the great strength that only comes from knowing the Source of that strength—God.

Singing songs about Him, to Him, propels us into awe, faith, and hope. *"Faith is the substance of things hoped for, the evidence of things not seen"* (Heb. 11:1). Our focus and gaze upon the infinite God enlarges and expands our view of Him, as all else fades and becomes small and insignificant in comparison. Remember we are singing about God. All of our concerns, problems, sins, weaknesses, and failures are nothing paralleled to beholding God! This is our God *"Who has measured the waters in the hollow of His hand, measured heaven with a span and calculated the dust of the earth in a measure? Weighed the mountains in scales and the hills in a balance?"* (Isa. 40:12). This is the God, while overwhelmed by awe, of who Job declared, *"I have heard of you by the hearing of the ear, but now my eye sees you"* (Job 42:5). He encountered the majesty of God. Seeing God is the beginning, the end, and the center of everything. God is looking at us, waiting for us to look at Him. I look forward to the day when all songs are birthed from seeing God. So let's sing about *Him!*

Third, we are invited to sing *spiritual songs*. This is specifically speaking about singing in the spirit, which includes singing in your spiritual language, called tongues, and also songs God gives you in your understanding. These are new songs inspired by the Holy Spirit.

Praying and singing in tongues focuses us on God rather than our needs. The spiritual gift of tongues makes a great impact on us, reaching our inner self as it bypasses our intellect and circumstances. There is something so powerful and mysterious—yet glorious.

> *I will pray with the spirit, and I will also pray with the understanding. I will sing with the spirit, and I will also sing with the understanding* (1 Corinthians 14:15).

I have found that in my own life, doing these three things is the quickest way for the Spirit to break into my calloused heart and for me to experience the empowerment and a fresh filling of the Holy Spirit.

When I start my prayer time praying in tongues, this usually leads me to singing my own melodies overflowing from my heart straight to the heart of God. I love making up my own melodies. Even though I would not describe myself as "musically inclined," when I was a child, I used to do this on a regular basis. This is so natural that you don't have to teach a child to do this. All of my children, whether they are musically inclined or not, make up their own melodies and sing their own songs with whatever is bubbling up out of their heart. Sometimes you feel dry and do not have anything good bubbling out of your heart, and that is one reason why you need the Scriptures or pre-written songs (hymns).

In the chapter called "Search for Him," I shared a powerful truth that I want to bring us back to: "What comes into our minds when we think about God is the most important thing about us."[12]

So let's look at our God in Scripture to establish how essential this is for our lives, as we were made in God's image.

And I heard a voice from heaven, like the voice of many waters... (Revelation 14:2).

Our God is a musical God with a majestic sound like the voice of many waters. Can you imagine what He sounds like? God is a melodic God who made us the same way. In fact He rejoices over us with singing (see Zeph. 3:17). So when our spirit comes into agreement with the living God within us, a great mystery is discovered. Doing these practices will help you be filled with the Spirit of God regularly and discover this great mystery within. Connecting and communing with God, singing melodies and singing Scriptures, are glorious and mysterious—this is how to facilitate being filled to the brim with the Spirit of God. I invite you to partake of this divine invitation!

I trust you are encouraged and provoked to start each day with a fresh filling of the Holy Spirit. I invite you to do this even now. Sing Psalms (Scripture and songs in Scripture), hymns (pre-written songs), and spiritual songs (singing in tongues and Holy Spirit-inspired songs), make melodies in your heart to the Lord and watch your life be transformed!

CONTINUAL STRENGTHENING BY THE HOLY SPIRIT'S POWER

As I end this chapter I want to pray a prayer that the apostle Paul prayed over the church. This is a prayer that I pray over my own life and those around me regularly. As I pray this, I am calling upon God's bountiful richness to empower you today!

That He would grant you, according to the riches of His glory, to be strengthened with might through His Spirit in the inner man, that Christ may dwell in your hearts through faith; that you, being rooted and grounded in love, may be able to comprehend with all the saints what is the width and length and depth and height—to know the love of Christ which passes knowledge; that you may be filled with all the fullness of God (Ephesians 3:16-19).

Father, I come before You on behalf of this reader, and I pray that You would provide him or her, according to Your rich, overflowing glory, with Your supernatural might and strength. I pray that You would strengthen his or her inner self! Overflow in this reader's life; awaken him or her to Your love to comprehend the depths of Your great love! Fill and strengthen Your child today. I pray great grace would abound in this person's life. In Jesus' name, Amen.

Chapter 11

FILLED TO OVERFLOWING

*We are no good if we only have a full cup. We
need to have an overflowing cup all the time. It's
a tragedy not to live in the fullness of overflowing.
See that you never live below the overflowing tide.*
—SMITH WIGGLESWORTH,
Smith Wigglesworth on Spiritual Gifts

What's the difference between all other religions and Christianity? I
remember arguing this point in the streets of Minneapolis while sharing
my faith. I was 16 years old and I would go to uptown or downtown
Minneapolis in hopes of seeing someone give his or her life to Jesus.
Many people I encountered wanted to know the difference between
thousands of other religions and Christianity. I remember getting into
discussions about whether or not Jesus really existed, what gender God
was, why do bad things happen to good people, and many others topics. People acted as if there was a supermarket of religions and beliefs
that all led to God—and they just needed to choose whichever one they
felt was right. Because of these mindsets and my youth, I didn't even
know where to start or where to go half of the time in my discussions
with people.

Although I have grown in my knowledge of sharing Christ, the confusion that encircles the search for God remains. In fact, I would say the confusion and wrong mindsets have only escalated. Many are embracing the philosophy that all religions and beliefs actually lead to the same place. This is presented in a variety of ways from widely known television hosts, movie stars, musicians, and even pastors of large churches. This ideology directly comes against the fundamental Christian truths that there is a narrow road to heaven (see Matt. 7:14), that God is the Judge of all of our actions and words, and that humankind has rebelled against the one true God and humanity has become God's enemy. The truth is that we need the Savior—and Jesus is the way.

Ravi Zacharias, in his book *Jesus Among Other Gods,* confirms, "Our society is becoming more and more 'pluralistic,' accepting all religions not only as alternative options but as equally correct views of life. Anything you believe sincerely enough, religious pluralistics say, will get you to God—and to heaven. You might hear it said like this: 'It doesn't matter what you believe—just that you believe it strongly.' 'Every faith leads to God.' 'All religions teach the same things.'"[1]

I want to emphasize that *not* all religions are the same, and that *only one* road leads to heaven. Even if you practice morally good habits, that doesn't mean your heart is good. Nor does that mean you're going to heaven because you have less "speeding tickets," so to speak, than the next person.

The difference between all other religions and Christianity—which, I would add, is not practiced by all who call themselves Christians—is a *relationship with a living God who can only be accessed through Jesus Christ.* This is so enormously significant that no other religion can compare to Christianity just on that point alone. There are other religions, but only one leads to God. Jesus said, *"I am the way and the truth and the life. No one comes to the Father except through me"* (John 14:6 NIV). Every other god is an idol that cannot see and cannot hear.

The Father, Son, and Holy Spirit are three Persons, yet one God—and He is alive. What an incredible thought! Our God is not dead! Jesus is alive! But it doesn't stop there. The best part of Christianity compared to all other religions is that the invitation to know God intimately is available to all who will take hold of it, as stated many times in this book. God created us for communion with Him. He doesn't want to rule us as if He were a dictator and needing to feed His ego, treating us as insignificant and existing only to serve Him; no, He wants to commune with us.

Many so-called Christians believe what I just said, but don't practice it. "A recent Gallup poll reported that 94 percent of Americans claim to believe in God or a universal spirit. However, a quick glance at Scripture and our culture makes it plainly obvious that nowhere near 94 percent actually know God. I mean really know him—intimately. Belief isn't the same as personal knowledge."[2]

Understanding to Inspire

The point of this entire book is to emphasize the importance of knowing God and living our lives the way God intended, from the inside out. I have also taught throughout this book what I consider to be my own elementary understanding of who God is, hopefully bringing a new perspective that brings alignment in our lives that allows us to view God differently, if we in fact have had a wrong view of Him. I laid out the perspective that God is the God of goodness and gladness; I illustrated the roles and operation of the Father, Son, and Holy Spirit in hopes of inspiring you to commune with God for yourself.

My desire in writing this is to see you live a Holy Spirit-led life, knowing God for yourself and living a vibrant life from the inside out. If we fail to have this as a reality in our lives, what is the point? Seriously, what is the point of being a Christian if we don't practice God's presence in a daily and real way? I don't want to simply be part of a club, even if it's a moral club. I don't want to simply have a place to go on Sunday or just half-heartedly give some time and money to a religious institution. I don't. I want God. I want Him! I want the reality that I was intended to have all along, and I want to live the way I was meant to live here on earth; it's a great mystery, but it's our true identity. *"Christ in you, the hope of glory"* (see Col. 1:27 NIV).

SOMEONE BETTER

Nevertheless I tell you the truth. It is to your advantage that I go away; for if I do not go away, the Helper will not come to you; but if I depart, I will send Him to you (John 16:7).

I always wondered why Jesus left to heaven after He rose. I was a little envious of the disciples because they were able to physically walk with Jesus for three years. Jesus says, however, that it is better for us to have His Spirit. Imagine that? He wanted us to have Someone better than Him being with us physically, or I should say among us. He wanted His Spirit to be in us for a constant, real communion. Now that's what I am looking for, the God who wants to be with me, not looking to punish me and make me pay some penance for my waywardness, as He is portrayed by so many. I simply want God. Humankind is searching and looking for the real God.

I have traveled to many nations and experienced many cultures. One thing has been common in seeing these other cultures and religions— the incessant need to have to pay for their failures and earn their way to their god. Humankind wants to rid themselves of their guilt and will do most anything, such as pay money, light candles, crawl on the ground, bow at certain times and perform various rituals. They seem to follow any person or set of requirements as long as they are promised forgiveness of sins and even the sins of family members, both future and present.

Humanity is searching for God and longing to know Him and be accepted by Him. One great truth that humankind is searching for is to know that God wants them—and He does. God wants me. He wants you. That is why He created us. He wants us more than we want Him, and He has proven that time and time again. *"If we are faithless, He remains faithful; He cannot deny Himself"* (2 Tim. 2:13).

BANQUET TABLE TO FEAST ON GOD

You prepare a table before me... (Psalm 23:5).

I have asked many friends how they keep their hearts alive before God throughout the various seasons of life. This is so important to me that I often make it a point of conversation. I also make sure that I seek to learn from others who write about their journey with God and watch and learn how they live. I want to become a student on how to maintain vibrancy on the inside of me that comes from a steady diet of feasting on God.

Growing in the experiential knowledge of God through regularly encountering Him is synonymous with growing in intimacy with God. As I stated earlier, I am most intimate with those whom I know the most; it is also true of you. Therefore, the more I know about and relate to a person, the more intimate I am with them. This is not a purely academic knowing. When I speak of growing in the knowledge of God, I am speaking of growing in the intimate knowledge of how He feels, thinks and acts, through encountering Him, experiencing Him, and not just memorizing facts about Him. God is not merely an object we can acquire information about, even though many live their lives doing this. God is a Person who is to be known. We study and grow in the intimate knowledge of God like we would a flower or a sunset; we observe, we drink in. And even more than a sunset or flower, we can talk and communicate. We can have friendship and a deep intimacy. This is what we are invited to.

There are three stages of growing in intimacy with God:

First it begins with the *invitation (menu):* His desire for dynamic relationship with us at a deep heart level (see Mark 3:13-15, John 15:16).

Secondly growing in intimacy requires *substance or knowledge of Him and responding to the invitation:* At the "heart of intimacy" is the relational knowledge of a Person (see John 14:23; 16:13).

Thirdly this deep interior pleasure and fascination will *overflow and produce* lasting character development and radical selflessness.

I have gone to many oceanfronts around the world. We can go to the same ocean and yet have a completely different experience than someone else. One person may visit the ocean, see the waves from afar and take photos. I have seen many who experience the ocean like this. For this person, it is true that they went to the ocean. Another person may go to the same oceanfront and take walks on the beach, collects shells and feel the water on their feet and sand in their toes. They also went to the ocean. Yet another person, invests their time, money and energy to get equipped, so they can descend into the depths of the same ocean and experience the wonders and beauty of what lies beneath the waters for themselves. The same is true of knowing God. Some are content to merely read and memorize the scriptures, knowing things about Him. Others remain content to simply feel the benefits of God in their life (healing, prosperity, and salvation), but fail to descend into the depths of knowing God. Yet I want to say there is so much more and we have an invitation to descend into the depths and really know

Him, and to do this we must live from the inside where God has taken residence![3]

A New Orientation

What I believe God is calling every one of us to is a new orientation—a new way of living where the inner self with a vibrant spirit affects the outer self. Spiritual growth occurs as our primary orientation for life makes a shift from natural experiences (our physical appetites, senses, and emotions) to our spirit.

There is a great mystery that takes place when we give our lives wholly to Jesus. The Holy Spirit (life Himself!) comes and we become born again. John 6:63 says, *"It is the Spirit who gives life."* This is supernatural life that we get from the inside. Our spirit comes alive as the Holy Spirit comes and resides in our spirit. This is mysterious and glorious all at the same time. This is the way forward in the Christian life. In Scripture the terms "to be led by" and "walk in" the Spirit are how we are to live from here on out.

If you study Romans 8, you will see how many times the word *spirit* is used. It goes back and forth from defining the Spirit of God and the spirit of man. Paul calls us to live according to the Spirit of God living in our spirit. This is fascinating to ponder and think about and then live out.

Watchman Nee, in his book *The Breaking of the Outer Man and the Release of the Spirit,* says:

> The Holy Spirit resides in our spirit, but it is difficult to tell which is the Holy Spirit and which is our spirit. There is a distinction between the Holy Spirit and our spirit, but the two are not separate. Hence, the release of the spirit is not merely a release of man's spirit but a release of the Holy Spirit through man's spirit, because the two spirits are one. We can differentiate the two spirits as terms but not in fact. The release of the

spirit is the release of the human spirit. It is also the release of the Holy Spirit. When others touch our spirit, they are touching the Holy Spirit at the same time.[4]

This truth is so fascinating to me. It's a complete mystery. First Corinthians 6:17 confirms this by stating that *"he who is joined to the Lord is one spirit with Him."*

This truth also is why praying for people, through the laying on of hands is so powerful. The laying on of hands is one of the doctrines of the Bible given to us in Hebrews 6:2—*"the doctrine of... laying on of hands."* This is one of the six fundamental principles that God wants us to live by. This practice in many places has been lost and forgotten, yet so fundamental to the early apostles who led by example.

> *But if the Spirit of Him who raised Jesus from the dead dwells in you, He who raised Christ from the dead will also give life to your mortal bodies through His Spirit who dwells in you* (Romans 8:11).

Derek Prince, in his book *Foundational Truths for Christian Living,* reveals, "Here the phrase 'to give life to your mortal bodies' means to impart divine life and power to the mortal, physical body of the believer in whom the Spirit of God dwells. The great agent of the Godhead who imparts this divine life is the third Person, the Holy Spirit."[5]

Laying on of hands is that point of contact where the power of the Holy Spirit is released through us. When this happens we transmit God's power for whatever is the need at hand. This is divine partnership of body, soul, and spirit; but best of all it's the transmitted power of the Holy Spirit through you and me.

LIVE BY THE SPIRIT

For those who live according to the flesh set their minds on the things of the flesh, but those who live according to the Spirit, the things of the Spirit (Romans 8:5).

We are to *"live according to the Spirit"* by living according to what *the Word* says concerning who we are in our spirit as we are *in Christ.* We are to live with *awareness* of our born-again spirit that has been made righteous by *dialoguing* with the *indwelling Spirit,* especially *thanking Him* for love, joy, peace, patience, and self-control that is in our spirit because of the Holy Spirit (see Gal. 5:22-23).

We are to live our lives set on the things of the Spirit. Now don't be fooled—our lives are always, continually focused on something or someone. The question is what? Is it on the Person of the Holy Spirit, or is it on the things of the flesh? We have to be intentional and focused on what we set our affections, time, and energy. This is what it means to set our minds on the things of the Spirit and to live there!

You see, we are invited to talk to God. The Christian life is an ongoing dialogue with a Person. He has much to say, but He allows us to set the pace of the conversation with Him. If we start the conversation, He will continue it as long as we do. When we stop it, He stops it and waits until we begin it again. He responds to the measure that we desire to talk to Him.

ABIDE IN CHRIST

Abide in Me, and I in you. As the branch cannot bear fruit of itself, unless it abides in the vine, neither can you, unless you abide in Me. I am the vine, you are the branches. He who abides in Me, and I in him, bears much fruit; for without Me you can do nothing (John 15:4-5).

This is one of the most profound invitations given by Jesus Christ to us: abide in Christ. We are invited to abide in Him. One thing I know is that whatever God asks us to do or invites us to, He provides the empowerment, or what the Bible calls *grace,* to help us in what He invites us to. If only we will take the invitation wholeheartedly, He will help us with that decision and give us the ability to do it.

This is the beginning point of deep connection with God that enables us to live in His presence in a much greater consistency than we ever knew possible. This can be sustained in all facets of life: in the marketplace, ministry, at home, on a sick bed, and even in prison. Once we taste a life of connectedness to the Spirit, we find deep pleasure. The pleasure of loving God is within the reach of all believers.

There are two components to our abiding in relationship with Jesus. *Our part* is in being faithful to turn our attention inward to communicate with the Spirit as the way of connecting with His presence in our lives. *God's part* is to release His supernatural activity within our hearts (our minds and emotions).

There is a great inheritance that we get to partake of when abiding in Him. Few know it, few comprehend it, and sadly even less will ever enjoy the fullness that there is in abiding in God. I am convinced that abiding and communing with God should be preached and taught with as much urgency and desire as the salvation message. We would grow into experiencing the fullness of God and bearing much fruit in every area of life if we abided in Him, and we would win the lost in a greater measure. I believe the second commandment to love our neighbor (see Mark 12:31) would flow naturally with such abundance out of abiding with Him.

It's quite the opposite right now. I see so much exertion in calling people to *do* for God, what should overflow out of love for God. You don't have to convince a lover that he or she should serve. You don't have to twist a lover's arm into giving out of his or her abundance or even to give sacrificially of finances, time, or affections. Lovers overflow. Lovers always out-give anyone else.

We were not only invited to come to God as just a means to be saved, we were invited to come to Him and stay with Him and to abide in Him. This was the very purpose for which He called us in the first place. You were meant to enjoy unbroken communion with Him.

Those who abide in Christ will bear much fruit in their lives. This speaks of experiencing intimacy with God and the supernatural power to have a vibrant heart. *Fruit* refers both to inward godliness, which is to have a vibrant heart in God (see Rom. 6:22; Gal. 5:22), and to touching people with the power of God.

INNER AFFECTING OUTER

He that believeth on me...out of his belly shall flow rivers of living water (John 7:38 KJV).

The way to live is truly from the inside out. So when the inner self overflows to the outward circumstances and touches many lives, including even our physical bodies, then we are living the way God intended from the beginning.

When we live the way I have laid out in this book—having a vibrant life from the inside, walking with the Holy Spirit, hiding His Word in us, and abiding in Him—it will overflow into touching people. Let me give an example. When we live life focused on outward circumstances and void of a life in God, we are like a dry sponge with no water. But when we live alive and vibrant, full of the Holy Spirit and the Word, we are like a sponge soaking up all the water we can. And as a sponge sitting in water is so full of water that when touched it leaks out water, so it is with us. The life of God just flows out of us.

POWER OVERFLOWING

Throughout history many men and women have affected their generations by the glory and power of God. A story that comes to mind is of John G. Lake, a great healing evangelist and missionary, who was a church planter and saw thousands healed by the power of God. One time in 1910, there was a dreadful plague in Africa where John G. Lake was stationed. Within a short time, one quarter of the population had died. John G. Lake offered to help, volunteering his time to bury the dead people. In this process John G. Lake was never affected with the very contagious plague; the doctors were amazed by this phenomenon.

> At the height of this horrible plague, a doctor sent for Lake and asked him: "What have you been doing to protect yourself? You must have a secret!" To this Lake responded: "Brother, it is the law of the Spirit of Life in Christ Jesus. I believe that just as long as I keep my soul in contact with the living God so that His Spirit is flowing into my soul and body, that no germ will ever attach itself to me, for the Spirit of God will kill it."
>
> Lake then invited the doctor to experiment with him. He asked the doctor to take the foam from the lungs of a dead plague victim and put it under a microscope. The doctor did so, and found masses of living germs. Then Lake astounded the people in the room as he told the doctor to spread the deadly foam on his hands and announced that the germs would die.
>
> The doctor did so and found that the germs died instantly in Lake's hand. Those who witnessed the experiment stood in amazement as Lake continued to give glory to God, explaining the phenomenon like this:

"You can fill my hand with them and I will keep it under the microscope, and instead of these germs remaining alive, they will die instantly."[6]

We are invited to know God for ourselves; and in turn as we know Him, we will impact nations and affect our generation as well as those in following generations.

THE LAW OF THE SPIRIT

There is therefore now no condemnation to those who are in Christ Jesus, who do not walk according to the flesh, but according to the Spirit. For the law of the Spirit of life in Christ Jesus has made me free from the law of sin and death (Romans 8:1-2).

What John G. Lake was operating in was the law of the Spirit that transcended the physical arena. You see, there are laws that govern the spiritual arena and laws that govern the physical realm. A law is consistent, unchangeable, and unwavering. In other words, whenever the same law applies to a certain set of conditions, the same outcomes result. For example, in the natural realm we have gravity. Gravity is a natural phenomenon that gives weight to objects, and even causes them to fall to the ground. This is a natural law that cannot be changed.

It's the same when it comes to the law of sin and death. We are not simply dealing with sin, but the law of sin. A person cannot fight the law of sin with human will. People need salvation, and only Jesus Christ can pay for this and redeem us from the law of sin and death. Many people live their entire lives by this law, but there is a better way to live. We are to live by the law of the Spirit.

Christianity operates on spiritual principles that transcend the laws of the natural universe. They rise above, go beyond, and exceed the natural laws of the universe. This means that when God preforms miracles, for example, He doesn't do away with the natural laws of the natural universe. He transcends them.[7]

The law of sin and death is there all the time, but God has put another law into operation—the law of the spirit of life in Christ Jesus. And that law is strong enough to deliver us from the law of sin and death. It is, you see, a law in Christ—the resurrection life that in him has met death in all its form and triumphed over it (Eph. 1:19-20). The Lord Jesus dwells in our hearts in the person of the Holy Spirit, and if, committing ourselves to him, we let him have a clear way, we shall find his new law of life superseding that old law. We shall learn what it is to be kept, not by our own insufficient strength, but "by the power of God" (1 Peter 1:5).[8]

POWER-FILLED GOSPEL

And my speech and my preaching were not with persuasive words of human wisdom, but in demonstration of the Spirit and of power, that your faith should not be in the wisdom of men but in the power of God (1 Corinthians 2:4-5).

Another great example of seeing the power of God at work is through the preaching of the Gospel. I have personally seen tens of thousands of people turn their hearts to God, young and old, male and female. I have always been amazed at the miracle of a person's heart turning toward God. I am a firm believer that it is not about how great an orator someone is. The preaching of the Gospel is not by Word alone, but by God's Spirit.

David Frost interviewed Billy Graham years ago on how he saw the Holy Spirit's role when it came to preaching the Gospel. Billy stated, "I believe that when the Gospel is preached, however badly or however many mistakes...the Holy Spirit is the communicatory agent; that people are really not listening to me after about ten or fifteen minutes if I'm really preaching the Gospel. I think they're listening to another voice inside, the voice of the Holy Spirit, and the Holy Spirit is applying and communicating."[9]

Another great present-day evangelist who moves with the supernatural power of God in his meetings is Reinhard Bonnke. Reinhard has had millions of people attend his meetings with many corresponding miracles, signs, and wonders. At one of Reinhard's first evangelistic meetings God spoke to him about preaching the Gospel. God said to Reinhard, "My words in your mouth are just as powerful as they are in my mouth."[10] This is not to brag about how great Reinhard Bonnke or Billy Graham are, but how great God is who can use a weak person willing to open his or her mouth and speak God's message.

The supernatural power of God always communicates the Word of truth to the heart. God desires us to partner with Him and His Word to preach the Gospel to the heart of humanity. The Word of God spoken is the chariot in which the Holy Spirit embarks upon with the destination of the human heart. The Holy Spirit never acts without the spoken Word; therefore speaking the Word of God activates the Holy Spirit to move!

HOLY SPIRIT UNCTION

What we need in this hour is Holy Spirit-anointed preaching. We need the Holy Spirit's unction to be upon our lips. There are many people who stand, preach, and present the Gospel, but there is a great chasm between a preacher who speaks, even eloquently, and those who speak with unction. I would also suggest this to those who lead in worship. Songs are sung all of the time, but with very little oil of the Holy Spirit on them. We don't need pretty little songs anymore, we need a new song, sung with the unction of the Holy Spirit that breaks in with deliverance, freedom, and releases open heavens over whole communities.

E.M. Bounds, in his book on prayer, speaks about the unction of the Holy Spirit, "What of unction? It is the indefinable in preaching which makes it preaching. It is that which distinguishes and separates preaching from all mere human address. It is the divine in preaching; it makes the preaching sharp to those who need sharpness. It distills as the dew to those who need to be refreshed…it impregnates, suffuses, softens, percolates, cuts, and soothes. It carries the Word like dynamite, like salt, like sugar; makes the Word a soother, an accuser, a revealer, a searcher; makes the hearer a culprit or a saint, makes him weep like a child and live like a giant; opens his heart and his purse as gently, yet as strongly as the spring opens the leaves."[11]

You might be a student, a stay-at-home mom, a worship leader, a person in the marketplace, you might not be a preacher, but we are *all* called to preach. You are called to live a life of anointing and unction. When you walk this earth and you go about your day, you are called to influence—speaking truth to your children and making a difference to people in the workplace. And if you are a preacher, you need this unction more than anyone. Unction-less preaching is not preaching. Let's contend for the unction of the Holy Spirit to be upon our lives, no matter what arena of life we are in.

RESULTS OF ANOINTED PREACHING

The Spirit of the Lord God is upon Me, because the Lord has anointed Me to preach good tidings to the poor; He has sent Me to heal the brokenhearted, to proclaim liberty to the captives, and the opening of the prison to those who are bound (Isaiah 61:1).

There is nothing like preaching the Gospel with supernatural, anointed power, which is the result of a life set apart, and being led by the Spirit of God. The Holy Spirit anticipates the Word of God to be spoken. The Spirit of God creates the theater for action.

I have read many accounts from history of great revivals and great moves of God. There are many things that occur such as physical manifestations, healings, miracles, even practical things such as crime rate dramatically changing and supernatural growth of produce—but the end result is people turning their hearts toward God. One of my favorite accounts is from Charles Finney, one of the most anointed preachers in history. One particular time he was invited to speak spontaneously in the city of Sodom. He didn't know the name of the city when he first arrived, and he didn't know the name of the gentleman who invited him. The gentleman's name just so happened to be Lot. This town named Sodom was not accustomed to having religious gatherings, so this was very rare. God told Finney to speak on Abraham and Lot from the Bible. This is Charles' account of what took place:

> I had not spoken to them in this strain of direct application more than a quarter of an hour when all at once an awful solemnity seemed to settle down upon them. The congregation began to fall from their seats in every direction and cry for mercy. If I had had a sword in each hand I could not have cut them off their seats as fast as they fell. Indeed, nearly the whole congregation were either on their knees or prostrate in less than two minutes from this first shock that fell upon them. Everyone who was able to speak at all prayed for himself.[12]

There was so much sobbing unto God that Finney could hardly talk to Lot, the man who invited him. This is an account of the Holy Spirit moving upon the spoken Word that cuts to the heart. The most calloused man is broken at the very real, tangible presence of the Holy Spirit. I have personally been in meetings like this where all desire is for God and the cry of people's heart is for forgiveness of sins and the knowledge of being made right with God. The cry is for "mercy"—and God is mercy. He is the only One who can provide mercy, forgiveness, freedom, and satisfaction for the soul. Charles Finney knew it wasn't him—it was God. Finney went on to say about that meeting, "My heart was so overflowing with joy at such a scene that I could hardly contain myself. It was with much difficulty that I refrained from shouting and giving glory to God."[13]

From Where Does Anointed Preaching Come?

Anointed preaching that pierces hearts only comes from a life of prayer and intimacy with God. The questions are: How do you get it? And how do you keep it? It is a conditional gift only taken hold of from a life of prayer and spending time before the Lord in prayer.

E.M. Bounds has some profound insights that I believe will challenge us to the core: "Only praying hearts are the hearts filled with this holy oil; praying lips only are anointed with this divine unction, prayer, much prayer, is the price of preaching unction; prayer, much prayer is one, soul condition of keeping this unction, without unceasing prayer the unction never comes to the preacher. Without perseverance in prayer, the unction, like manna over kept, breeds worms."[14]

The anointing has to be fresh; therefore prayer has to be daily and continual in order to receive it and have anointed preaching and an anointed life.

Receive the Holy Spirit

Then they laid hands on them, and they received the Holy Spirit (Acts 8:17).

If you are like me, then you want to experience and live by all that God has for you on this side of heaven. Jesus Christ ascended to heaven for us to have the promised Holy Spirit and to walk continually filled with Him. In order to walk full of the Holy Spirit, we must receive Him and His empowerment!

In Acts 8:17, all the disciples did was lay hands on the new believers and the believers received the Holy Spirit. "Interestingly, *lambano* (Greek, "receive") conveys both the ideas of giving and receiving. In short, everything ultimately relates to our willingness to be open to Him, to allow His power, grace and glory to flow all ways—to and from us!"[15]

I invite you to partake of God's divine nature by receiving the Holy Spirit to fill you and anoint you to overflowing. I urge you to ask the Father to touch you afresh with the baptism of the Holy Spirit.

> *But you shall receive power when the Holy Spirit has come upon you; and you shall be witnesses to Me in Jerusalem, and in all Judea and Samaria, and to the end of the earth* (Acts 1:8).

Jesus called His disciples to wait for the promised Holy Spirit so He would come upon them for the purpose of being His witnesses. The disciples were waiting, with expectancy, to be baptized with the Holy Spirit; or another way to describe it would be for the immersion of the Holy Spirit. Without being baptized with the Holy Spirit, there would be little or no purpose or power in being His witness.

Today, no one has to wait for the Holy Spirit. That was the call for those disciples in that day because the Holy Spirit had not come yet. The promised Holy Spirit has come now, and He is here now ready to touch you and fill you to overflowing. All you have to do is posture your heart and life to receiving Him and welcoming Him.

OVERFLOWING

> *Now may the God of hope fill you with all joy and peace in believing, that you may abound in hope by the power of the Holy Spirit* (Romans 15:13).

God's purpose is to inhabit us, fill us, and overflow from us. He wants us to experience and encounter Him in a real tangible way forever. And from this place, He desires to immerse us so that we overflow with the river of God's life and power touching many lives. As we abide and commune with God, there will be an overflow of peace and joy. This is the most glorious way to live.

I pray that as you have read this book, you are inspired to live from the inside out, with the Spirit of the living God penetrating your spirit and overflowing from you. I will say it again as I have said all the way through this book—*there is no other way to live in the fullness of God, than living from the inside out!*

ENDNOTES

INTRODUCTION

1. A.W. Tozer, *The Pursuit of God* (Camp Hill, PA: Wing Spread Publishers, 1982, 1993), 50.

CHAPTER 1

1. Thomas Dubay, *The Evidential Power of Beauty* (San Francisco, CA: Ignatius Press, 1999), 17.
2. Stephen Venable, "Mystical Life of Communion, Session 1: Vision for Communion—the Relevance of Intimacy," 7, International House of Prayer eschool, http://www.ihopkc.org.
3. Stephen Venable, "Mystical Life of Communion," 6.
4. Stephen Venable, "Mystical Life of Communion," 11.
5. Stephen Venable, "Mystical Life of Communion," 13.
6. J.I. Packer, *Knowing God*, (Downers Grove, IL: InterVarsity Press, 1993), 35.
7. A.W. Tozer, *The Knowledge of the Holy* (Fig Books, Electronic Edition), 2.
8. Stephen Venable, "Mystical Life of Communion," 14.
9. Matt Candler, "The Way to Intimacy, Session 1: The Bridal Paradigm, Part 2," 1, International House of Prayer eschool, http://www.ihopkc.org.
10. Stephen Venable, "Mystical Life of Communion," 13.

11. Bible Study Tools, s.v. "desire," http://www.biblestudytools.com/dictionary/desire/.

12. Matt Candler, "The Way to Intimacy, Session 14: Hunger & Thirst, Pt. 2," 4, International House of Prayer eschool, http://www.ihopkc.org.

13. Stephen Venable, "Mystical Life of Communion, Session 4: Indwelling of the Holy Spirit," 1, International House of Prayer, eschool, http://www.ihopkc.org.

14. Richard J. Foster, *Celebration of Discipline* (New York: HarperCollins Publishers, 1998), 24.

15. Misty Edwards, "Garden," Forerunner Music 2007

CHAPTER 2

1. A.W. Tozer, *The Purpose of Man: Designed to Worship* (Ventura, CA: Regal From Gospel Light, Kindle Edition, 2009), 30.

2. Misty Edwards, *What Is the Point?* (Lake Mary, FL: Passio, Charisma Media/Charisma House Book Group, 2012), 8.

3. Ibid., 7.

4. Ibid., 9.

5. A.W. Tozer, *The Purpose of Man: Designed to Worship*, 42.

6. A.W. Tozer; edited by James L. Snyder, *Experiencing the Presence of God* (Ventura, CA: Regal From Gospel Light, 2010), 50.

7. A.W. Tozer, *The Purpose of Man: Designed to Worship*, 43.

8. Robert S. McGee, *The Search for Significance* (Nashville, TN: Thomas Nelson, 1988), 18.

9. Keith Krell, *"Grace to the End," Bible.org,*, http://bible.org/seriespage/grace-end-1-thessalonians-523-28.

10. Ibid.

11. Andrew Wommack, "1 Thessalonians 5:23," Andrew Wommack Ministries, http:// www.awmi.net/bible/1th_th05_23.

12. Derek Prince, *Expelling Demons* (Grand Rapids, MI: Chosen Books, 1988), 159.

13. Andrew Wommack, *Spirit, Soul and Body*, (Tulsa, OK: Harrison House, 2010, Kindle Edition), 66.

14. Ibid., 178.

15. Ibid., 229.

CHAPTER 3

1. John Piper, "*Love Your Neighbor as Yourself,* Part 2," Desiring God Ministries, http://www.desiringgod.org/resource-library/sermons/love-your-neighbor-as-yourself-part-2.

2. John Piper, *Desiring God*, (Colorado Springs, CO: Multnomah Books, Kindle Edition, 2011), 215.

3. Blaise Pascal, *Pascal's Pensees,* trans. W.F. Trotter (New York: E.P. Dutton, 1958), 113.

4. Jonathan Edwards, *Safety, Fullness and Sweet Refreshment, To Be Found in Christ,* in Jonathan Edwards on Knowing Christ, (Edinburgh: Banner of Truth, 1990), 166.

5. J.I. Packer, *Knowing God*, (Downers Grove, IL: InterVarsity Press, Kindle Edition, 1973), 43.

6. Sam Storms, *Pleasures Evermore*, (Colorado Springs, CO: NavPress, Kindle Edition, 2000), 42.

7. John Piper, *Desiring God*, 290.

8. Sam Storms, *Pleasures Evermore*, 78.

9. Ibid., 50.

10. Sam Storms, Pleasures Evermore (Colorado Springs, CO: NavPress, Kindle Edition, 2000) 50.

11. Foster M. Olive, *Ecstasy (Understanding Drugs),* (New York: Infobase Publishing, Kindle Edition, 2010), 149.

12. Ibid., 353.

13. Mike Bickle with Deborah Hiebert, *The Seven Longings of the Human Heart*, (Kansas City, MO: Forerunner Books International House of Prayer, Kindle Edition, 2006), 254.

14. Ibid., 265.

15. Sam Storms, *Pleasures Evermore*, 56.

16. A.W. Tozer, *The Purpose of Man* (Ventura, CA: Regal From Gospel Light, Kindle Edition, 2009), 43.

CHAPTER 4

1. J.I. Packer, *Knowing God* (Downers Grove, IL: InterVarsity Press, 1973, Kindle Edition, 1973), 15.

2. Ibid., 21.

3. Ibid., 25.

4. A.W. Tozer, *The Knowledge of the Holy* (Fig Books, Electronic Edition, 2012), 2.

5. Ibid., 8.

6. John Bevere, *Drawing Near* (Nashville, TN: Thomas Nelson, 2004), 61.

7. Allen Hood, "The Book of Daniel, Session 10," 9, International House of Prayer eschool, http://www.ihopkc.org.

8. Allen Hood, "The Book of Daniel, Session 1," 15, International House of Prayer eschool, http://www.ihopkc.org.

9. A.W. Tozer, *The Knowledge of the Holy*, 114.

10. Ibid., 115.

11. Mike Bickle, "The Beautitudes: The Only Way to Happiness and Greatness," International House of Prayer, http://www.mikebickle.org.

12. Misty Edwards, *What Is the Point?* (Lake Mary, FL: Passio, Charisma Media/ Charisma House Book Group), 41.

13. Ibid., 40.

14. Brother Lawrence, *The Practice of the Presence of God* (New Kensington, PA: Whitaker House, 1982, Kindle Edition), 313.

15. Corey Russell, *Pursuit of the Holy* (Kansas City, MO: Forerunner Books, 2006), 83.

16. A.W. Tozer, *God's Pursuit of Man* (Camp Hill, PA: Wing Spread Publishers, 1978), 8.

17. A.W. Tozer, *The Knowledge of the Holy*, 1.

CHAPTER 5

1. Dictionary.com, s.v. "father," http://dictionary.reference.com/browse/father.

2. John Eldredge, *Fathered by God* (Nashville, TN: Thomas Nelson Inc., 2009).

3. Jack Hayford, *Explaining the Trinity* (Lancaster, United Kingdom: Sovereign World LTD, 2003, Kindle Edition), 381.

4. Ibid., 396.

5. Floyd McClung, *The Heart of the Father* (Eugene, OR: Harvest House Publishers, 1985), 19.

CHAPTER 6

1. A.W. Tozer, *The Knowledge of the Holy* (Fig Books, Electronic Edition, August 2012), 22.

2. Corey Stark, "Jesus Christ, The Glorious Man," Corey Stark Ministries, http://www.coreystark.com.

3. John Piper, *Seeing and Savoring Jesus Christ* (Wheaton, IL: Crossway Books, 2004), 119.

4. Ibid., 166.

5. Ibid., 172.

6. Ibid., 175.

7. Ibid., 190.

8. A.W. Tozer, *The Knowledge of the Holy*, paraphrased quote, 1.

9. Mike Bickle, *Jesus, the Son of Man (Rev. 1), Part 6 of the series Jesus, Our Magnificent Obsession Part 1,* www.mikebickle.org, October 23, 2011, 1.

10. A.W. Tozer, *From the Library of A.W. Tozer*, comp. James Stuart Bell, (Bloomington, MN: Bethany House, 2011), 183.

11. Ibid., 183.

12. Ibid., 210.

13. Brother Lawrence, *The Practice of the Presence of God* (New Kensington, PA: Whitaker House, Kindle Edition, 1982), 256.

CHAPTER 7

1. Allen Hood, *Baptism of Holy Spirit and Fire*, Pursuit Conference, Alberta, Canada, 2011.

2. A.W. Tozer, *Life in the Spirit* (Peabody, MA: Hendrickson Publishers Marketing, 2009), 5.

3. Ibid., 6.

4. Ibid.

5. Ibid.

6. Ibid., 7.

7. John Bevere, *Drawing Near* (Nashville, TN: Thomas Nelson Publishers, 2004), 141.

8. Andrew Murray, *The Essential Works of Andrew Murray* (Uhrichsville, OH: Barbour Publishing Inc., 2008), 404-405.

9. Mike Bickle, "Fellowshipping with the Holy Spirit," International House of Prayer, http://www.mikebickle.org (posted April 2008).

CHAPTER 8

1. Joyce Meyer, *Power Thoughts: 12 Strategies to Win the Battle of the Mind* (New York: Faith Words, E-book Edition, 2010), 3.
2. James Allen, *Mind is the Master: The Complete James Allen Treasury* , comp. Jeremy P. Tarcher, (New York, NY: Penguin Group, Kindle Edition, 2010), 2877.
3. Ibid.
4. Ibid., 2867.
5. Mike Bickle, "The First Commandment, Part 4: Loving God with All Our MInd," International House of Prayer, http://www .mikebickle.org.
6. John Piper, *Think: The Life of the Mind and the Love of God* (Wheaton, IL: Crossway, 2010), 1117.
7. James Allen, *Mind is the Master: The Complete James Allen Treasury,* 9387.
8. Ibid., 9396.
9. C. Samuel Storms, *Signs of the Spirit: An Interpretation of Jonathan Edwards' "Religious Affections,"* (Wheaton, IL: Crossway, 2007), 199.
10. Corey Russell, *Ancient Paths: Rediscovering Delight in the Word of God* (Shippensburg, PA: Destiny Image Publishers, 2012), 86.
11. Richard J. Foster, *Celebration of Discipline* (New York: HarperCollins Publishers, 1998), 24.

CHAPTER 9

1. Mike Bickle, "Cultivating the Oil of Intimacy," International House of Prayer, http://www.mikebickle.org. Starts at 52 minutes into the presentation.
2. Billy Humphrey, *Until He Comes* (Kansas City, MO: Forerunner Publishing, 2009), 28.

3. Ibid.

4. Isaac Bennett, "Speech: The Overflow of the Heart," International House of Prayer, Kansas City, http://3. amazonaws.com/ihopkc-marketing/resources/Speech-The +Overflow+of+the+Heart+-+Isaac+Bennett+113012.pdf.

5. Corey Stark shared a personal dream, with his interpretation and application, which I fully endorse.

6. Mike Bickle, "Ephesus: Returning to Our First Love (Rev. 2:1-7)," Forerunner School of Ministry, http://www.mikebickle.org.

7. Ibid., 4.

8. Corey Russell, *Ancient Paths* (Music CD: Burning & Shining Lamp Ministries, November 19, 2010), ASIN: B004D4YF8W.

9. Leonard Ravenhill, *Why Revival Tarries* (Bloomington, MN: Bethany House Publishers, 1987), 25.

CHAPTER 10

1. Richard J. Foster, *Prayer: Finding the True Hearts True Home* (New York: HarperCollins Publishers1992), 7.

2. Richard J. Foster, *Celebration of Discipline: The Path to Spiritual Growth* (New York: HarperCollins Publishers, 1992), 33.

3. E.M. Bounds, *The Complete Works of E.M. Bounds on Prayer* (Grand Rapids, MI: Baker Books, 1990), 369.

4. Jack Hayford, *Living the Spirit-formed Life* (Ventura, CA: Regal Books, 2001), 265.

5. Corey Russell, *The Glory Within: The Interior Life and Power of Speaking in Tongues* (Shippensburg, PA: Destiny Image Publishers, 2011), 73.

6. John Bevere, *The Holy Spirit: An Introduction* (Palmer Lake, CO: Messenger International, 2013), 2349.

7. Ibid., 2367.

8. A.W. Tozer, *Tozer on Worship and Entertainment* (Camp Hill, PA: Wingspread, 1997), 67.

9. Ibid., 72.

10. Ibid.

11. Ibid.

12. A.W. Tozer, *The Knowledge of the Holy* (Fig Books, Electronic Edition), 1.

CHAPTER 11

1. Ravi Zacharias and Kevin Johnson, *Jesus Among Other Gods* (Nashville, TN: Thomas Nelson, Youth Edition, Kindle Edition, 2000), 5.

2. Craig Groeschel, *The Christian Atheist* (Grand Rapids, MI: Zondervan, Kindle Edition, 2010), 33.

3. Corey Stark, "The Glory of Encountering God in the House of Prayer," Corey Stark Ministries, http://www.coreystark.com.

4. Watchman Nee, *The Collected Works of Watchman Nee, Volume 54* (Anaheim, CA: Living Stream Ministry, Kindle Edition, 1994), 2496.

5. Derek Prince, *Foundational Truths for Christian Living* (Lake Mary, FL: Charisma House, 2006), 345.

6. Roberts Liardon, *God's Generals: Why They Succeeded and Why Some Failed* (New Kensington, PA: Whitaker House, 1996), 183.

7. Roberts Liardon, *School of the Spirit*, (Cheshire, England: Faith Builders World, Kindle Edition, 2012), 1350.

8. Watchmen Nee, *The Normal Christian Life* (Wheaton, IL: Tyndale House Publishers, 1977), 188-189.

9. David Frost, *Billy Graham: Personal Thoughts of a Public Man* (Colorado Springs, CO: Chariot Victor Publishing, 1997), 63.

10. Christian Broadcasting Network, "Interview with Reinhard Bonnke, March 29, 2013," viewed on YouTube, http://www .youtube.com/watch?v=d6EWyBKypr4.

11. E.M. Bounds, *The Complete Works of E.M. Bounds on Prayer* (Grand Rapids, MI: Baker Books, 1990), 479.

12. Charles Finney, *The Autobiography of Charles Finney* (Bloomington, MN: Bethany House Publishers, 1977), 82.

13. Ibid

14. E.M. Bounds, *The Complete Works of E.M. Bounds on Prayer,* 482.

15. Jack Hayford, *Living the Spirit-Formed Life* (Ventura, CA: Regal Books, 2001), 265.

ABOUT ANTONIO BALDOVINOS

Marked by boldness and passion, Antonio Baldovinos has an uncompromising message of calling the Church to a whole-hearted pursuit after God. Since 2000, Antonio has traveled to many nations seeing tens of thousands respond to the Gospel. In 2008, God expanded his vision to call people to a lifestyle of prayer and intimacy with God. It is this passion that brought him and his wife to establish the Global Prayer House Missions Base, which includes the Pursuit Conference, the Pursuit Internship, and the Pursuit Worship, all flowing out of the place of prayer and worship. Antonio and his beautiful wife, Christelle, live in Alberta, Canada, and love raising their five children: Michael, Gabriel, Elijah, Isabella, and Justice.

Contact Information

Website: www.antoniobaldovinos.org

Email: info@antoniobaldovinos.org

Twitter: @Antoniobaldov

For more about Antonio's ministry, visit the following websites:

Global Prayer House: www.globalprayerhouse.com

Pursuit Conferences: www.pursuitmovement.com

Pursuit Internship: www.pursuitinternship.com